Venice
osterie

Michela Scibilia

Venice
osterie

bars, wine bars,
trattorias, restaurants
a handbook for
discriminating diners

Vianello
LIBRI

concept, design, text, photographs, maps, graphic design, layout and the like
Michela Scibilia

editors
Elisabetta Ballarin
Andrea Montagnani
Nicolò Scibilia

english translation
Giles Watson

editorial consultant
Livio Scibilia

fonts and symbols
Scala sans (Martin Majoor, 1993)
Shop (Michela Scibilia
with Elisabetta Ballarin, 2004)

printed by
Grafiche Vianello
Treviso

Special thanks to Daniele
Resini for allowing the author
to make frequent use of his
superb digital camera, without
which this guide could not
have been completed.

This guide is dedicated
to inquisitive restaurateurs
who eat at other people's
establishments and pay the
occasional visit to bookshops.

advisors and companions at table
Chiara Barbieri
Annabella Bassani
Ilaria Boccagni
Vito Bon
Isabella Bonora
Marie Brandolini
Monica Briata
Catherine Buyse Dian
Maria Giulia da Sacco
Luca d'Este
Marina Errera
Elena Fumagalli
Gael Greene
Luca Grinzato
John and Sue Laithwaite
Alessandra Magistretti
Girolamo Marcello
Marta Moretti
Claudio Nobbio
Cesare Polano
Augusto Rillosi
Carole and Dick Rifkind
Marco Saba
Marco Scurati
Brian Sexton
Adrian Smith
Gaia Stock
Roberto Tonini
Manuel Vecchina
Mara Vittori
Laura Zuccolo

and all the unfortunates
at the next table whose
opinions I extorted

and all those who have sent
me their observations and
travel notes over the years.

Eateries featured are offered
spontaneously as personal
suggestions. This guide is not
an official publication for the
promotion of trade or tourism,
nor is it supported by
sponsorship of any kind.
The publisher and author
decline any liability, of whatever
nature and for whatever reason,
for the information and data
contained in the guide.
Just to make things clear.

Please note that the editorial
policy outlined above means
that we cannot accept paid
advertisements.
Comments and suggestions
from readers are very welcome.
(info@teodolinda.it – please
indicate "Venice Osterie"
in subject line).

This guide is published every
three years or thereabouts.
Updates to the current edition
can be downloaded from
www.teodolinda.it/osterieup.

Version 4.1
Febbruary 2006

contents

presentation

You can't eat out all the time.

That might seem a slightly unusual way to start a guide to eateries in Venice but it is undeniable that sitting down at a restaurant table is a game of chance few of us can afford to play. It might be the economy, the euro, the price of oil or the shifting migration routes of herons, but everything costs too much. Unsurprisingly, eating out costs even more in Venice. Let's just do one or two sums. A full sit-down meal of starter, pasta, main course, side dish and dessert, excluding drinks, at a good – not exceptional, mark you – restaurant will come to about fifty euros a head. That's one hundred euros for two. For a lot of people, that means almost two whole days' earnings. As a result, a lot of people simply don't go out to eat.

But there must be a solution, as we wait for better times, because eating in company is one of life's greatest pleasures. And it's an even greater pleasure in Venice. So what can we do? Well, we can adopt one of the following alternative strategies. Strategy number one is "sip and run". You have a glass of something nice and nibble a cichèto *in an attractive* osteria, *or at a table in the* campiello *if the weather's nice. This shouldn't cost you more than four or five euros. Take your time and then skip merrily home to a nice plate of spaghetti, either on your own or with someone agreeable. Strategy number two is "little but good". You go out for a meal once every other month, but choose the best places and don't count the pennies.*

The third strategy is "keep a low profile". You get organised, keep up to date and discover the right places at the right prices. You may not always swoon at the food on offer, but if your friends are congenial, you'll still have a great evening. You could probably afford this once a week or so.

Strategy number four is "lunchtime is the right time". At midday, many restaurants offer tempting menus at prices that if not always cheap are certainly much more economical than in the evening. Why not take advantage?

But whatever your strategy, this guide, now in its fourth edition, is sure to be useful. The criterion used for selecting the eateries is as scientific and objective as it was in earlier editions – my personal taste. In other words, these are the places I go to eat out, and where top-quality food is prepared with care and commitment.

If the quality is in the local tradition and promotes the local territory, so much the better, but this is not mandatory.

As usual, this guide also aims to offer variety.

You'll find variety in cooking styles, which range from traditional Venetian to ethnic and fantasy-inspired fusions. There's variety in the categories, too, from osterie that might do you half a boiled egg, but have superlative cellars, up the scale to top-flight restaurants with menus of Rabelaisian proportions.

As we have mentioned, prices also vary. There are the big name establishments, and which actually deserve their big names, alongside others with less wallet-crippling prices. Sadly, "cheap" is no longer part of my vocabulary.

But my palate was not the only criterion for inclusion in this guide.

Thanks to the "where I like to go" rule of thumb adopted, there are also places where the food may not be stunning but the view certainly is. An indifferent meal tastes a whole lot better in a perfect setting. Other places may have a marvellous garden or a big dining room where you can take the kids. In yet other cases, the focus may be on the oste, the sometimes curmudgeonly creator who runs the eatery and builds the rapport with diners. In short, I have tried to pin down the special something there is in – almost – all of these eateries that makes them stand out from the crowd.

In comparison with the previous edition, there are a number of new, often excellent "sip and run" osterie. In contrast, there are not many new sit-down restaurants. Often, these are an evolution of the classic restaurant concept in the sense that they are lighter, albeit not in price. But they will let you enjoy a glass of good wine and a single, often far from run-of-the-mill, dish or perhaps a selection of cheeses in the peace of an inner courtyard or a deck in the campo. It seems that to some extent,

"CRAB CLAWS"
CRAB-FLAVOURED FOOD PRODUCT MADE FROM SURIMI (RECONSTITUTED FISH). ONE VERSION IS COLOURED ORANGE AND SHAPED INTO A CRAB'S CLAW BUT THE PRODUCT IS MORE FREQUENTLY FOUND BREADED AND DECORATED WITH A REAL CRAB'S CLAW. VENETIANS CALL THE SECOND TYPE A POLPÉTA CO' L'UNGHIA (FISHBALL WITH A NAIL).
WOULDN'T IT BE MORE HONEST – AND HEALTHIER – JUST TO SERVE PLAIN OLD FISH FINGERS?

the impulse to eat tempting food in company in an attractive setting is gaining
the upper hand over the desire for a full meal with all the trimmings.

For this edition, an effort has been made to find eateries that in a more normal city
would be called transport cafés, the sort where you can find honest-to-goodness home
cooking at a reasonable price. There are still a few around, and Venetians watch over
them jealously. They are the last remaining places where you can eat for not much
more than ten euros. Hard as it might be to believe, Venetians are normal people who
work in normal offices and usually have a normal lunch hour to fill. These endangered
eateries are crucially important. Often, though, they are only open at midday, or only
have transport-café prices at lunchtime. Read the comments carefully.

In almost all cases, I offer suggestions on what to order. Even a very good restaurant
may have a less successful dish, and there is always a risk of plunging your fork into it.
One recent fashion is raw fish, such as tuna, sea bass, scampi and even cuttlefish or
scallops. I love raw fish but nowadays it is as widely available as it is poorly prepared. —9
It can be delicious, but it can also be a huge disappointment.

It is also our sincere wish that bar counters, even in good osterie, will no longer feature
crab "claws" made from reconstituted fish, potato croquets, Ascoli-style stuffed and
fried olives and other offerings that have come straight from the freezer yet are passed
off as traditional Venetian cichèti. Many traders have jumped on the "tradition equals
quality" bandwagon and the results are catastrophic. Presenting a crab claw as a
traditional cichèto, or a vase made in China as Murano glass, is no less than criminal.
Instead of creating added value, it drains the lifeblood from Venetianness, leaving only
the hollow shell of the name. This sets off a chain reaction, to the detriment
of Venetians who put their hearts and souls into their work.

To round off this brief introduction, here are three hints and a wish.

Hint one is to read the comments carefully, and between the lines if necessary.

Number two is always book ahead, otherwise you might end up walking several
kilometres for nothing.

Hint three is forget about Saturday evening.

And my wish is that Venice Osterie will help you to discover Venice's living, beating
heart, where good people do a good job well, and good eateries serve good food.

I hope you will be able to say that "it really is still possible to eat out in Venice!"

Michela Scibilia

where to meet

Rialto ▶ B

Now that the Erbaria fruit and vegetable market, previously for wholesalers only, has been opened to the public again, Venetians have a superb terrace right on the Grand Canal. With the adjacent *campo*, it is now one of the city's liveliest districts. There are four good *osterie* – Naranzaria, Bancogiro, Marcà and Muro – in a radius of a hundred metres and crowds of young people gather every evening. There are no homes around the Erbaria, just offices, so you might stumble on an open-air concert. You can linger till late in the evening without risking a bucket of water from an irate would-be sleeper on an upper floor. In the neighbouring *calli* are recently and not so recently established *osterie*, all traditional in style (Do mori, Do spade, all'Arco and ai Storti).

Campo San Bartolomeo and Campo San Luca ▶ D

10— This can be the setting for a pleasant evening stroll, even if it is part of the city's most tourist-infested routes. Since the Erbaria opened, many people have moved over to the far side of the Rialto, but there are still good *osterie* to be found here, as well as lots of friendly company to make sure you don't have to go to bed too early. Starting from San Bartolomeo, pop into alla Botte for an aperitif, then ai Rusteghi for a filled roll and a glass of good red. On your way to Campo San Luca, you can have something to eat at a la Campana and chat late at Vitae, the place for night owls. In the reverse direction, starting from Campo Santo Stefano, you can kick off with a *cichèto* at Fiore and a *sprìtz* at all'Angolo before working your way up to the San Bartolomeo area.

Zattere ▶ G

The embankment facing the Giudecca is a favourite with Venetians who want to stretch their legs. Sitting down over a coffee to flick through the paper on a fine winter's morning is one of life's simple pleasures. If you are out and about in the afternoon, call at Nico's or even better at the Squero a little way along Fondamenta Priuli.

In the evening, the dreamy atmosphere will work its magic on just about any member of the female sex, making it the destination of choice for romantically involved couples, or new friends who intend to get that way. There are lots of restaurants on the embankment but they are all over-priced and just a touch too touristy.

Those looking for a pre or post-stroll plate of spaghetti and a salad won't go far wrong at the ever-reliable *osteria* San Basilio. If you have a bit more spare cash and want a fantastic panorama with your meal, Linea d'ombra right at the other end is just the place.

Fondamenta della Misericordia and Fondamenta degli Ormesini ▶ A

Another traditionally busy area that attracts young people who are a bit *sciòpai, sciòpai*
types who are no longer young, and thirty or forty-somethings looking for a good time.
The eateries here are all lined up along the *rio*. You will find ethnic cuisine (Sahara),
sit-down meals and traditional *cichèti* bar snacks (Rioba, Bea vita e Bacco), as well as
something a little trendier (al Timon). In summer, there may be a moored barge with
music. In the evening, don't forget the Fondamenta della Sensa, which runs parallel and
where you will find the Anice stellato and ai Quaranta ladroni.

Via Garibaldi ▶ E

Just when you've got used to Venice's *calli, fondamente* and *rii terà*, you discover there
are some exceptions, like long, straight Via Garibaldi. Until less than a century ago, it too
was a canal. After it was infilled, it became the hub of a very working class area where
you can find Venice's most characteristic fauna, although the nearby Biennale gives it a
cosmopolitan air during the summer. There are plenty of bars and restaurants.
On Via Garibaldi itself is al Garanghélo and ai Tosi Piccoli is tucked away among the *calli*. ⎯11
You could have a *sprìtz* in one and an evening meal in the other.

Campo Santa Margherita ▶ F

One of Venice's biggest, and in the evening most vibrant, *campi*. There are a number
of university departments in the area so it is frequented mainly, but not exclusively, by
students. As you nudge your way through the groups of youngsters, you can drift from one
bar to another, although none, with the exception of Do draghi, is really special. Nearby
Calle dei Preti, just past San Pantalon, is another busy district. If you want to have an
evening meal, it's worth continuing to Calle Lunga San Barnaba, where you have a choice
of several restaurants: Oniga, Quatro feri, la Bitta, San Barnaba, Avogaria and at the far
end, Pane vino and San Daniele.

Strada Nuova ▶ B

Strada Nuova is an avenue that was evidently drawn with a ruler, which is most un-
Venetian. The *rii terà* that continue its course to the railway station are also sometimes
improperly referred to as Strada Nuova. It's always busy, generally because people there
are heading somewhere else, but in the midst of all the *forèsti*, students, office workers,
porters and shopkeepers, you can find a few good *osterie*. You'll be able to nibble a *cichèto*
or have lunch (Ca' d'Oro), a serious *sprìtz* (il Santo bevitore), a glass of wine and a decent
crostìno (la Cantina) or a proper evening meal (Vini da Gigio, al Portego del pescaor,
da Bepi già 54, al Vecio bragozzo).

Frequently Asked Questions

or tasty snippets to get you started

Where can I find a really traditional *osteria*?
Da Dante.

Any other *osterie* with wooden tables, paper napkins, a *cichèto* counter and hot food?
da Alberto, Anice stellato, Bacco, Bea vita, Botte, a la Campana, Ca' d'Oro, Cravate, il Diavolo e l'acquasanta, ae Do spade, al Garanghélo (1 and 2) da Pinto, Portego, Ruga Rialto, ai Storti and Vivaldi.

Where do they serve the best *cichèti*?
All'Arco, la Cantina, un Mondo divino and al Prosecco.

Where can I get a serious glass of wine?
All'Aciugheta, al Bancogiro, Cantina, Cavatappi, alla Mascareta, un Mondo divino, Naranzaria, al Prosecco, ai Rusteghi, Vinus and Wine bar.

Which restaurants have the best-stocked cellars?
The Fiaschetteria toscana and da Fiore are in a class of their own. Then you should try agli Alboretti, al Covo, Corte sconta, San Marco, Santa Marina, Vini da Gigio, alle Testiere and Vino vino. On the mainland, da Mariano, la Pergola, la Ragnatela, Ombre rosse, da Caronte and da Conte are all excellent.

Where do I go for a traditional fish dinner in a serious restaurant with white tablecloths and all the trimmings?
Alla Madonna, da Ignazio, or the restaurants on Burano and Pellestrina.

MOÉCA

Which establishments have stayed more or less the same since
the first edition twelve years ago?
Only twenty-four out of the original one hundred and thirty: all'Aciugheta, Antiche
carampane, all'Arco, Algiubagiò, da Bes, alla Botte, Corte sconta, al Covo, da Dante, Fiore,
da Fiore, Fontana, Harry's Bar, alla Madonna, al Nono risorto, da Pinto, Gislon, ai Rusteghi,
alle Testiere, Ca' d'Oro, Vini da Arturo, Vini da Gigio, Vino vino and alla Zucca.

Which places have opened recently, or are under new management?
Altrove, Antico giardinetto, Aurora, ai Artisti, Avogaria, al Bacaro, Barbarigo, Bea Vita,
Boccadoro, Centrale, alla Ciurma, ae Cravate, al Garanghélo (1 and 2), Linea d'ombra, un
Mondo divino, Muro, Naranzaria, Pane vino e San Daniele, Santo bevitore, ai Storti, al
Timon, Vecio Forner and Vinus.

What about non-Italian cuisines?
Mirai (Japanese), los Murales (Mexican), Ganesh hi (Indian), Frary's bar
(Mediterranean/Middle Eastern) and Sahara (Syrian).   _13

Where can we meet for an aperitif?

exclusive	Harry's bar, Monaco – Gran canal
scenic	Algiubagiò, Angiò, Bancogiro, Linea d'ombra, Naranzaria
traditional	Aciugheta, all'Angolo, all'Arco, alla Botte, Cantinone, Do mori,
	Do draghi, Fiore, alla Mascareta, Muro, Rusteghi, Vitae,
	Ca' d'Oro and Cavatappi
alternative	Altrove, Bacaro, Baffo, Birraria, Centrale, da Lele,
	ai Storti, Rivetta, da Dante, Mondo divino and Wine bar

Dove xe che magna i murèri?
In other words, where do building labourers – and others who want a filling meal without
having to remortgage the house – go to eat?
Cea, Due gondolette, dalla Marisa, Mistrà, Palanca and Tre scaini.

And what about a pizza with the gang from school?
Algiubagiò, Nono risorto, Birraria, al Faro and ai Tosi piccoli.

We want to eat a pizza in a scenic spot that will really make us feel on holiday.
Acqua Pazza and il Refolo.

Where do you suggest for Sunday lunch?

Acquapazza, agli Alboretti, Anice stellato, Angolo di Tanit, Antico giardinetto, Avogaria, Bandierette, al Bacco, Bea vita, da Bepi - già 54, Birraria, Boccadoro, al Covo, al Diporto, al Faro, Fiaschetteria toscana, al Fontego dei pescaori, Frary's Bar, al Garanghélo, ai Gondolieri, Harry's bar, da Ignazio, Linea d'ombra, alla Madonna, da Mario, dalla Marisa, Mistrà, Monaco – Gran canal, al Nono risorto, Oniga, Pane vino e San Daniele, ai Quaranta ladroni, il Refolo, Rioba, dai Tosi piccoli, Tre spiedi – da Bes, Vecio bragozzo, Vecio fritoin, Vini da Gigio, Vino vino and Vivaldi.

What do Venice's big shots go?

Antiche carampane, da Fiore, Harry's bar, Vini da Arturo, Vini da Gigio, da Fiore and da Ignazio.

... and where do the local gourmets eat?

agli Alboretti, Corte sconta, al Covo, Fiaschetteria toscana, ai Gondolieri, Santa Marina, Vini da Gigio and alle Testiere.

... and for a quick lunch in the San Marco area?

a la Campana, Leon bianco, Vino vino or Vitae.

Can you suggest somewhere intimate for dinner à deux?

Agli Alboretti, alle Testiere, Monaco, Vini da Gigio and la Bitta.

Which restaurants can you take an – oared – boat to and find somewhere to moor?

Anice stellato, da Baffo, al Bancogiro, Canottieri, Cantinone – già Schiavi, Fontana, al Fontego dei pescaori, Frary's bar, da Lele, dalla Marisa, il Refolo, Rioba, Rivetta, Sahara, Vini da Gigio and alla Zucca.

Where can you go with a big group?

Alla Madonna, Ruga Rialto, Corte sconta, Birraria or Nono Risorto.

Which places keep the kitchen open from midday until night time?

San Marco and alle Vignole.

Where can you find something to eat and drink late in the evening?
da Baffo, alla Mascareta, Centrale, Bacaro, Do spade, Cavatappi, Vitae, al Timon, Ruga Rialto, Sahara, Do draghi, Muro, Naranzaria, Pane vino and San Daniele

Who are the meat specialists?
la Bitta, ai Gondolieri, Vini da Arturo and dalla Marisa.

What places have a good selection of sweets?
Fiaschetteria toscana, da Fiore, Santa Marina, Vini da Arturo and alla Zucca.

Where can we sit outside with plenty of space to enjoy a drink in the open air?
Angiò, al Bancogiro, da Baffo, la Cantina, ai Do draghi, Prosecco, Naranzaria and Linea d'ombra.

... and for an al fresco meal?
Acquapazza, Boccadoro, Canottieri, al Diporto, Fontana, da Ignazio, dalla Marisa, il Refolo, Rioba and Sahara.

Why not go for a *giro di ombre* (an *osteria* crawl)?
It doesn't require much organisation. Start early, at about half past six. Almost all the *osterie* close before nine in the evening and the ones that offer restaurant facilities close the bar. Then just follow your nose round the bars, enjoying an *ombra* and a *cichèto* at each stop...

At Rialto: al Marcà, al Muro, alla Ciurma, all'Arco, ai Do mori, ai Storti and da Pinto.

At Cannaregio: Ca' d'Oro, ai Osti, alla Cantina, al Santo bevitore, Do colonne and Pontini.

SPRITZ

Where can you eat well without breaking the bank?
Good question.

the eateries
of Venice ...

legend

☞   Good value for money.

[€ 32] ✗   Trattoria/restaurant or similar establishment where you can eat a full meal at table, in a dignified manner. For eateries in this category, the average cost in euros of a full meal is indicated in brackets. The figure includes starter, pasta, main course, side dish, sweet, table charge and service but excludes wine and other drinks. A similar system has been applied to the *osteria*-style establishments. The prices quoted may look excessive but it should be remembered that customers will usually order only one or two dishes.
With very few exceptions, kitchens in Venice are open at more or less the same time (12.30 pm–2.30 pm and 7.30 pm–10.30 pm). Other times mentioned refer to bar service. Unless otherwise indicated, the kitchen will observe the usual hours.

♆   It is possible to have just a drink at the bar.
Often, bar service is suspended during kitchen hours.

🍾   Well-stocked cellar.

☀   Tables inside and al fresco.

★   Particular attention paid to quality and freshness of ingredients. Food is professionally prepared.

🛴   Children welcome. Ambience, service and type of menu offered ensure adults and smaller guests can co-exist. Note that it is always better to eat out with children at midday. But don't expect to find high chairs or baby changing areas.

🔍   Eatery that has opened or changed management recently. We have indicated only those establishments that have made a promising start and whose enthusiasm deserves encouragement. As these entries are the most likely to be altered, they are indicated by a special symbol.

♥   One of the author's favourites. This symbol is not an indication of quality as all the locales in the guide have been selected for – almost entirely – objective reasons. It simply denotes a personal preference.

in italics   Venetian and Italian terms included in the glossary on page 82.

all'Aciugheta [€ 54] ♟ ✕ 🍾 ▶ D, E

041 5224292, Castello 4357,
Campo Santi Filippo e Giacomo
⊙ 12 am–3 pm and 6–12 pm, open all week

A bar, *enoteca*, restaurant and pizza restaurant that is a classic stop on any *giro di ombre*, although
its recent history has been at times puzzling. Avoid the tourist-filled tables and head for the counter
to enjoy a *polpetta*, a *crostino* or some of the excellent cheeses.

You might prefer a nice hot mini-pizza with anchovy, perhaps washed down with a glass of one of the
many fine wines from Gianni's well-stocked cellar. The modern new adjoining room is now popular
with locals on their lunch break, who generally eat a single course and head back to the office, but you
can snack and drink at the bar here, too. We renew our approval as we await future developments.

Acquapazza [€ 78] ✕ ☀ ★ ▶ D

041 2770688, San Marco 3808, Campo Sant'Angelo, closed Monday

Antonio has brought the flavours and simpatia of Naples to the Venetian
lagoon. His fluffy pizzas are really good, if a tad on the expensive side
(€ 11 and up). The fresh tomato and buffalo mozzarella pizza is unmissable
but there are plenty of other good things, such as pepper-baked mussels,
salmon with onions and capers, batter-fried vegetables (yummy), bucatini
pasta with scorpionfish, linguine with lobster, stuffed squid and grilled or
steamed *mazzancolle*. The bread and fresh pasta are made on the premises,
as are the inventive fruit sorbets. As a final touch, you can enjoy your meal
under white awnings in one of Venice's brightest and most central *campi*.

da Alberto [€ 32] ✗ ♟ ⚒ ▶ B

041 5238153, Cannaregio 5401, Calle Giacinto Gallina
🕐 10.30 am–3 pm and 6–10 pm, closed Sunday

Located between Campo Santi
Giovanni e Paolo and the beautiful
Miracoli church, this *osteria*-trattoria
provides refreshment in comfort for
customers from Venice and elsewhere.
The counter is well stocked with
fried sardines and *baccalà*, excellent
meatballs, shrimp, and boiled *latti di
seppia*. In winter, there's *nervéti* with
onion and *muséto*, and *castraùre* in springtime.
If you want to sit down, you can choose from
a range of pastas, risottos and *pasticci* with
fish or shellfish and vegetables, mixed seafood
fries, grilled fish, steamed cuttlefish and
baccalà with *polenta*. This is a good place to
come if you're in a hurry and just want a quick
plate of something for lunch.

agli Alboretti [€ 63] ✗ ♟ ☀ ★ ▶ F

041 5230058, Dorsoduro 882, Rio Terà Antonio Foscarini, closed Wednesday and Thursday morning

If you want to impress someone special, then bring your guest here. Situated right next to the
Accademia, agli Alboretti offers you a cool terrace, good service and fine cuisine in an elegant, slightly
retro setting. Quality and freshness are guaranteed and the kitchen pays great attention to matching
ingredients and balancing flavours. Sauces and spices exalt without smothering. Try *mazzancolle* and
asparagus with a lime and vanilla emulsion, velouté of carrots with fillet of mackerel in black sesame
seeds or cockerel supreme in a semolina crust with nettle quiche. The cheese board will delight
aficionados, as will the wine list, which lavishes particular attention on meditation wines and grappas.

Algiubagiò [€ 25/56] ✕ ♟ ☀ ▶ B

041 5236084, Cannaregio 5039, Fondamenta Nove ● 6.30 am–11.30 pm, closed Tuesday

Bounding Venice to the north are the Fondamente Nove, where ferries leave for Murano, Burano, Torcello and the airport. At Algiubagiò, you can contemplate the lagoon from the generous terrace as you watch commuters and tourists come and go. The menu at this bar, restaurant and pizza restaurant is long, ranging from sandwiches to full meals. We suggest you start with a bracing *sprìtz*, then try the

20_ grilled beef, Aberdeen Angus, reindeer or duck, or perhaps a pizza. The large wood and brick dining room was stylishly restored by Murano-born Davide Barbini.

Altanella [€ 50] ✕ ☀ ▶ G

041 5227780, Giudecca 268, Calle delle Erbe, closed Monday and Tuesday

Stefano in the kitchen and Roberto, who serves at table, are fourth-generation restaurateurs who continue the fine tradition of this small eatery on the Giudecca, near the Palanca waterbus stop. Much loved by Venetians in search of a little peace and quiet for its homely atmosphere and leaf-shaded gravel terrace, Altanella also has those crucial three hundred metres of water between its tables and the rest of Venice.

The small but carefully selected menu has everything you could wish from a traditional Venetian eatery, including baby octopus in oil and lemon, *sardèle in saór*, *gnocchi* with cuttlefish, bean and *polenta* soup, grilled fish or *figà a la venexiana*.

Altrove 🍷☀ ▶D

041 5289224, San Polo 1105, Campo San Silvestro
🕐 7.30 am–1 am, closed Sunday

Campo San Silvestro is off the track normally
beaten by tourists, despite being big, very central
and only a stone's throw from the ever-busy
Rialto and Riva del Vin. The recently opened
Altrove is popular with Venetians, particularly
young mothers who come here on the pretext of
taking the kids out and then stop off for a *spritz* and a look around. It's also a pleasant
place for a plate of cold meat with pink grapefruit and rocket, or a nice *tramezzino*.

da Alvise [€ 55] ✕☀ ▶B

041 5204185, Cannaregio 5045, Fondamente Nove, closed Monday

Take a seat at one of the strategically placed tables
on the pavement and soak up the view of the
northern lagoon. You can see the islands of Vignole
and San Michele, Murano and on a clear day the
majestic backdrop of the Alps. Apart from the view,
there are plenty of pizzas to enjoy (€ 6-10).
If you prefer something traditional, you might try
the sautéed cockles or cuttlefish cooked in their ink.
We recommend the chef's pasta. Order some
linguine with lobster, or shrimp and broccoli.
Don't forget to mop up the sauce with the

_21

delicious bread baked on the premises. It's too good to waste.

Angiò 🍷☀ ▶E

041 2778555, Castello 2142, Ponte della Veneta Marina
n 7 am–9 pm (in summer, until 12 pm), closed Tuesday

Giorgia and her brother Andrea run the only decent eatery
on the long, ultra-touristy and impossibly atmospheric

stretch of front that runs from
San Marco to the Arsenale.
This is the place for a
panoramic aperitif, if there
aren't too many boats tied
up outside, and the selection
of wines, cheeses and cold
meats is worth exploring.
Otherwise opt for a swift
lunch of filled rolls, salad or
tramezzini (the one with
hot sauce is fantastic) and
a glass of good Irish beer.

all'Angolo ♥ ☀ ▶ D, F

041 5220710, San Marco 3464, Campo Santo Stefano

◉ 6.30 am–9 pm (in summer, until 11 pm), closed Saturday

A favourite meeting place, not just for its strategic position but also for the friendly people who run it.
They are an excellent reason for coming here instead of some of its more pretentious neighbours.
The *tramezzini* are many and appetising, the *panini* are good and the *sprìtz* is the stuff of legend.
Enjoy all this as you look onto scenic Campo Santo Stefano.

l'Angolo di Tanit [€ 49] ✕ ♦ ♥ ★ ☀ ▶ A

041 720504, Cannaregio 1885, Calle dell'Aseo, closed Tuesday

Battista has done what he set out to do. He has turned a corner of northerly Venice into a little bit
of Sicily. So be prepared for swordfish roulades, spaghetti with pesto trapanese, made with fresh
tomatoes, garlic, basil, almonds and olive oil, wonderful pasta with sardines, fish couscous, caponata
made from eggplants, celery, tomatoes, onions, capers and olives in a sweet and sour dressing,
and tuna with citrus fruits. And *cannoli*, obviously.

Take the opportunity to sample some of the fine Sicilian wines and as you leave, loosening your belt,
cast an eye over the shop opposite that sells a refined range of Sicilian products.

Anice stellato [€ 44] ☞ ✗ ♀ ▮ ☀ ♥ ★ ► A

041 720744, Cannaregio 3272, Fondamenta della Sensa ● 10 am–3 pm and 6.30 pm–11 pm, closed Monday

A good place to eat and much loved by many because it does not suffer from the widespread
Venetian restaurateur's *ciaparli tuti* (grab 'em all) syndrome of raking in as much money as possible,
with double shifts and tables spilling off the decking. Fragrant herbs and aromatic spices grace the
tagliatelle with scampi and *fiori di zucca*, the fish risottes, the spaghetti with baby cuttlefish and
cannellini beans or sardines, bell peppers and balsamic vinegar, the baked salmon with potatoes and
lamb chops breaded in pistachios and potatoes. Round off with a cinnamon Bavarian cream with
plum and red wine sauce. The cuisine is creative and carefully prepared from meticulously chosen
ingredients. As a result, this small restaurant, tucked away on the lovely Fondamenta della Sensa
and run by a single, well-organised family, is a firm favourite with the locals. Be sure to book.
At the cocktail hour, a counter is laid out for *ombre* and *cichèti* and in the summer, you can
dine on the *fondamenta* itself, waving at the boats going up and down the *rio*.

Antiche carampane [€ 60] ✗ ♀ ☀ ♥ ★ ► B, D

041 5240165, San Polo 1911, Calle de le Carampane, closed Sunday and Monday

Let yourself be drawn into the maze of long, narrow *callette*, dark *sotopòrteghi*, courtyards and *rii terà*
that protect what was once the city's red-light district. If you had good directions, you will come to
this small eatery, an oasis of hospitality – apart from the irritating signs at the entrance – orderliness,
atmosphere and fragrant fish prepared with masterly skill.

Choose from *cassopìpa* (spaghetti with shellfish sauce), monkfish baked in foil with a crust of parmesan
cheese, marvellously delicate mixed fried fish or fresh spring vegetables. Follow up
with a mousse or Bavarian cream with seasonal fruits, such as figs, chestnuts or
persimmons. Recently, Antonia and Piera have been joined by
Francesco, who has brought with him the energy of youth. A fine eatery.

Informazioni
solo £ 5000
€ 2,50

Antico giardinetto [€ 60] ✕ ☀ ★ ▸ B
041 721301, Santa Croce 2253, Calle dei Morti, closed Monday

Venetians love restaurants that are close to home but sconti (hidden), just off the busy routes through the city. That is certainly one of the reasons why Lollo and Luca's recently opened restaurant has been such a success. The dining area is unpretentious but we should add that Lollo runs one of the best fish stalls in the Rialto market, which means the fish is always wonderfully fresh. The mixed starters, tuna tartare, grilled scallops and grilled fish in general are all prepared to the highest standards, although they are a bit expensive. There's a tasting menu at € 47 and for adventurous diners, a mixed platter of raw fish with everything from sea bass to cuttlefish.

Aurora ♟ ☀ 🐾 🔍 ▸ D
041 5286405, Piazza San Marco ◉ 7.30 am–1 am, closed Monday (also closed Tuesday in winter)

Piazza San Marco is Venice's most important district but the one least visited by Venetians themselves. There is, however, one fashionable spot with prices a shade lower than its neighbours where you will find the odd local resident. Breakfast costs € 8, spritz or a toasted sandwich € 6, and cocktails are € 12. Officially, at least. Random discounts may be applied, depending on whether you are Venetian, Italian, simpatico or just another tourist.

24_

all'Arco ♟♥ ★ ▸ B
041 5205666, San Polo 436, Calle dell'Occhialer ◉ 8 am–3 pm, closed Sunday

A postage stamp of an osteria near Rialto. The few tables in the calle are much sought-after during

shopping hours at the market or when it's time for an evening aperitif. The atmosphere is invariably cheerful and friendly. Francesco Pinto and his son Matteo serve up very good unbottled wines and above all some of the finest cichèti in Venice. There are delightful little panini, warm crostini with robiola cheese, mushrooms and salt meat, mini mozzarella in carrozza with anchovy, envelopes of asparagus and fiori di zucca filled with ricotta cheese and smoked speck ham, eggplant envelopes with ham and mozzarella. Connoisseurs will find traditional Venetian cichèti of spiénsa, tetìna or rumegàl. What a shame it's not open in the evening!

ai Artisti ▼☀ ▶F

041 5238944, Dorsoduro 1169a, Fondamenta della Toletta
🕐 8 am–10 pm, closed Sunday

Here on the busy *fondamenta* between Campo San
Barnaba and the Accademia, you can relax with a good
sprìtz and thumb through your purchases from the many
nearby bookshops. If you're hungry, choose one of the hot
dishes (€ 7-14) such as a nice plate of pasta, a steak or
a stew. Given the number of people popping in and out,
don't be surprised if you see someone you know before
you've finished your meal.

Avogaria [€ 63] ✕▼♦☀ ▶F

041 2960491, Dorsoduro 1629, Calle dell'Avogaria, closed Tuesday

This is the interior designers' eatery. Note the seriously sophisticated
styling, meticulous graphic solutions – even in the bathrooms – and
the conversation corner with comfy armchairs and small exhibitions by
up and coming designers. In fact, there's everything it takes to feel very
cutting edge. But don't expect nouvelle cuisine or the like because in the
kitchen Antonella reigns supreme, preparing mouth-watering concoctions

from Puglia, with one or two variations
of her own. There are pepper-baked
mussels, cavatelli pasta with cannellini
beans and cockles, orecchiette pasta
with Puglia-style sauce. Mimmo will be
happy to recommend a wine – some
are sold by the glass – from a list that,
as you might expect, has a wide range
of Puglian bottles, including Rosso
Salentino Armécolo. At midday, there is
a shorter menu and *cichèti* at the bar.

al Bacaro [€ 64] ✕▼ ▶D

041 2960687, San Marco 1345, Salizada San Moisè 🕐 9 am–2 am, open all week

Nowadays the only traditional thing about this eatery is the name,
bàcaro, but if you want to eat after midnight, it can be a good option.
Tucked behind the new Mondadori bookshops is this large, vaguely
hi-tech establishment offering skilfully made cocktails (€ 5-10)
to sip perched on the high bar stools.

On the floor above is a big glass and steel
restaurant where you can nibble warm
moscardini with celery and balsamic vinegar,
fillet of dory with artichokes and sherry, fillet
of sole with prosecco or thin-sliced beef
with aromatic herbs.
A full meal here can strain the wallet.

al Bacco [€ 47] ✗ ☟ ▸ A

041 717493, Cannaregio 3054, Fondamenta de le Capuzine
● 7 pm–11 pm (and 12 am–3 pm on Sunday), closed Monday

An utterly classic *osteria* with hot food, a warm welcome, big wooden tables, a wooden bar and wooden dressers. The equally traditional menu makes no concessions to fads or fashion. You'll find *sardèle in saór*, spaghetti *alla bùsara* or with cuttlefish, grilled fish and mixed fish fry. Round off your meal with *bussolài* and a glass of sweet wine, or a plate of *tiramisù*. Honest and reassuring.

da Baffo ☞ ☟ ☀ ▸ C

041 5208862, San Polo 2346, Campo Sant'Agostino ● 7.30 am–2 am, open all week

A busy, noisy beer and sandwich bar much beloved of students, young professionals and university lecturers who are still young at heart. The morning passes in a flurry of cappuccinos and croissants before office workers turn up in the middle of the day for a one-dish meal or a salad.

By early evening, the faces have changed. New ones continue to arrive until the wee small hours, when the clientele is generally sipping gin and tonics, mohitos or caipirinhas at a table in the airy *campo*.

Don't make too much noise, though. The neighbours are not night owls. There are chess sets, backgammon and dice for those winter evenings when groups of friends meet after a visit to the nearby cinema club for an evening of Burmese documentaries in the original language. Happy hour is 8 pm–9 pm on Sunday and Tuesday.

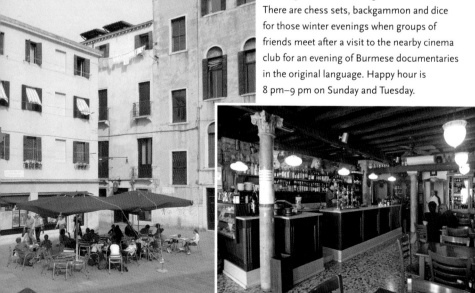

al Bancogiro ♥♦ ✳♥★ ▶B, E

041 5232061, San Polo 122, Campo San Giacometto
● 10.30 am–3 pm and 6.30 pm–12 pm, closed Monday

This *enoteca* beneath the porticos of the Fabbriche Vecchie
has two entrances. One is from the market and the church
of San Giacometto while the other, with tables, faces onto the
Canal Grande. Al Bancogiro stands on the site of one of Venice's, and perhaps history's, earliest trading
banks and has kept the original institution's name. You can stand at the bar, selecting your tipple from
the ten or so wines by the glass (the range of *cichèti* is limited). If you like, sit down at one of the tables
outside or in the cosy room on the first floor. You'll need to be a little patient since everything is made
to order, but you will be rewarded by the delights that Andrea and Elena dream up with the freshest
of ingredients from the nearby market (€ 12-14 each). Choose from prawns with *castraùre*, thin-sliced
raw *branzino* with a salad of fragrant herbs, fillet of turbot with yellow pumpkin and rosemary, creamed
sea bream, steamed fish salads or smoked American beef. Finish off with something from the small
selection of cheeses or a tempting sweet, such as baby ricottas with fresh figs and chestnut honey.

Bandierette [€ 34] ☞ ✗ ✳🛒 ▶E

041 5220619, Castello 6671, Barbaria de le Tole, closed Monday evening and Tuesday

This is a typical neighbourhood trattoria near Santi Giovanni e Paolo. Plain if not downright anonymous
on the outside, it is a firm favourite with local residents and well-informed holidaymakers. It's easy to

see why people come here.
The prices are affordable and
the genuine homestyle cooking
is perked up by a touch of
imagination. The fish-based
menu ranges from baked fan
shell scallops to fried sardines,
monkfish or grilled *branzino*.
The tasty pastas include
tagliatelle with scampi and
spinach, or spaghetti with
canòce or shrimps and
asparagus.

Barbarigo ☞ ✕ ☕ ☀ ⚲ ▶ D

041 5289758, Castello 5252, Santa Maria Formosa,
Fondazione Querini Stampalia ● 10 am–10 pm, closed Monday

Let's be intellectual for a moment.

Querini Stampalia is the students' favourite library,
a place where they can kid on they're studying until
midnight, or even on Sunday.

The bar inside is run by young people from the
Barbarigo catering school whose concoctions are

on offer at affordable prices (€ 9 each). You can try pasta, *pasticcio*,
chicken curry, lamb chops and meatballs in tomato sauce. The dining
area is lean to the point of bareness but on sunny days, they put a few
tables out in the courtyard-garden designed by Carlo Scarpa.

Bea vita [€ 54] ☞ ✕ ☕ ☀ ⚲ ▶ A

041 2759347, Cannaregio 3082, Fondamenta de le Capuzine ● 9 am–11 pm, open all week

Some time ago, three enterprising young men got together to open
this small restaurant, now a firm favourite with the food cognoscenti.

28_ Like most of the eateries on this long *fondamenta*, it has a table or two
outside, as well as a counter well stocked with *cichèti* and temptingly
good *ombre*. In the middle of the day, there is a nice, inexpensive menu
for local office workers and generous portions in the evening make the
well-prepared offerings very decent value. The price may look stiffish but
most people won't eat more than two courses. Try red mullet on a purée
of papaya with mint vinaigrette, *prosecco*-aromatised seafood risotto,
herb tagliatelle with lamb sauce and baby tomatoes or oven-baked baby
lobster with shellfish and grape sauce, and to round off, rhubarb mousse served in a pineapple basket
with maraschino. The wine list is carefully chosen, if not very long, but you can get wines by the glass.

For the time being, it's not too difficult to find a table.

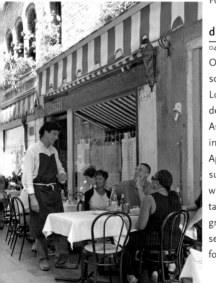

da Bepi – già 54 [€ 44] ✕ ☕ ♥ ☀ ▶ B

041 5285031, Cannaregio 4550, Campo Santi Apostoli, closed Thursday

One of Venice's long-term problems is a falling population,
so perhaps the city council should erect a monument to
Loris. He is attempting single-handedly to reverse the
demographic trend with his family of four boys and one girl.
As he waits for official recognition, he keeps himself busy
in his lovely trattoria a stone's throw from Campo Santi
Apostoli. The menu features classic Venetian fish dishes,
such as *canòce*, *caparòssoli*, seafood risotto and cuttlefish
with *polenta*, but there are also concessions to simpler
tastes, with *pasta e fasiòi*, *gnocchi* with tomato sauce or
grilled steak. This is a good place to spend a couple of hours
seated at one of the open-air tables, perhaps before heading
for the nearby cinema.

Birraria [€ 36] ✕ ♈ ☀ ✿ ▶ B, C, D

041 2750570, San Polo 2168, Campo San Polo ● 11 am–11.30 pm, open all week

In a Venice that has experienced a mini-boom in births
recently, it is not easy to find eateries that welcome restless
toddlers. But here, the menu is extensive and there is
something for everyone, from good pizzas to salads, pasta,
rice and meat (no fish). This is the place for a large families or
those groups that you pray you not to find at the next table if you're on a first date.
During the summer, the open-air tables dominate Campo San Polo, one of Venice's largest.

_29

la Bitta [€ 40] ☞ ✕ ♦ ☀ ▶ F

041 5230531, Dorsoduro 2753a, Calle Lunga San Barnaba ● 6.30 am–11 pm, closed Sunday

No fish here, but it's the perfect *osteria* for a satisfying meal in the dining room, or in the small internal
courtyard if the weather's nice. The menu is short but excellent, varying with the season and the
market as Marcellino explores the kitchen of the Veneto hinterland.
You may find *porcini*, potato *gnocchi* with pumpkin and smoked
ricotta cheese, roast Treviso pork with sea salt and rosemary,
shin of veal on the bone *in tècia*, chicken strips with chanterelle
mushrooms, duck in pepper sauce, *soprèssa de casada* (home-style
country salami), *radicchio di Treviso in saór*, linguine with white meat
sauce, stewed goose and *figà a la venexiàna*. There's a tempting
selection of cheeses served with honey and *mostarda*.
Debora will help you choose
a good wine by the bottle or
the glass.

Boccadoro [€ 58] ✕ ☀ ✈ ⚲ ▶ B

041 5211021, Cannaregio 5405a, Campiello Widmann, or dei Biri,
closed Monday

You'll need a good map to find Boccadoro and
its open-air tables in Campiello Widmann, but
when you get there, you can savour Luciano's
shortish but mouth-watering fish-based menu.
Choose from tartare of tuna, marinated
branzino, tagliolini with mussel sauce or fillet of
dory with courgette flowers. There are one or two
rather good wines on the list. Prices are perhaps
a shade ambitious. You may find swarms of noisy kids chasing each other round the *campo*.
Diners should refrain from using the cutlery to discourage them.

alla Botte [€ 37] ☛ ♦ ▶ B, D

041 5209775, San Marco 5482, Calle della Bissa ● 10 am–3 pm and 5.30 pm–11 pm,
closed Sunday evening and all day Thursday

Tucked away in a *calletta* near San Bartolomeo is a place where you
can sip a good aperitif with vaguely radical young people and the odd
older customer. After elbowing your way to the counter, you'll be able
to choose from thirty or so wines by the glass and a wide range of
polpette, potatoes, *folpéti* and other delights.

Hot food (€ 8-14) is on offer in the dining room. The selection
includes spaghetti with lobster, tagliatelle with scallops or scampi and
baby tomatoes, *figà a la venexiàna*, cuttlefish cooked in their ink or
tripe in parmesan cheese.

a la Campana [€ 17/48] ✕ ♥ ▶ D

+39 041 5285170, San Marco 4720, Calle dei Fabbri
● 12 am–3 pm and 7 pm–10 pm, closed Sunday

You won't find a more traditional-looking *osteria* than
a la Campana, from its dark wood walls to the paper
napkins, but the management is young and dynamic.
The menu at midday is less expensive, offering quick
meals – spaghetti with
tomato sauce, *pasticcio*,
stew – for workers from
the many offices in the
area. In the evening, there
is pasta with fish and
other sauces cooked to
order, traditional dishes
and a little more peace.
In other words, it's a safe
haven from the tourist-
driven chaos outside.

Ca' d'Oro – alla Vedova [€ 39] 🖙 ✗ ♥♥ ▶ B

041 5285324, Cannaregio 3912, Ramo Ca' d'Oro ● 11.30 am–2.30 pm
and 6.30 pm–11.30 pm, closed Thursday and Sunday morning

The best-known of the longer-established *osterie*,
perhaps because it has maintained its standards of quality. Obviously,
this makes it a must-stop for those enjoying a *giro di ombre* on the
Strada Nuova. *Forèsti* love its warmth, its atmosphere and the variety
of the *cichèti* Renzo and Mirella have on offer. There's a veritable
compendium of traditional Venetian cooking, with whitebait, *polpettine*,
folpéti cònsi, grilled, boiled and stuffed vegetables, *castraùre*, *fondi di
carciofo* (in season), *sardèle in saór, baccalà*, skewers of shrimp and *sépe
róste* (grilled cuttlefish). Select your *ombra* from the range of unbottled
wines. If you don't just want a quick snack, you can sit down to one
of the other specialties of the house – the spaghetti *alla bùsara* or in
cuttlefish ink are excellent – but it's advisable to book in advance.

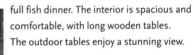

Canottieri [€ 20/44] ✗ ♥ ☀ ▶ A

041 717999, Cannaregio 690, Fondamenta San Giobbe ● 8 am–3 pm and 7 pm–11 pm, closed
Monday evening and Sunday (booking required in the evening in winter)

Canottieri used to be a relaxing bar – Venice peters out into the lagoon a few metres further on – but
since the area became yet another university colony, it throngs with students and building workers
attracted by the short menu of well-priced offerings at midday (€ 11-15). In the evening, you can have a
full fish dinner. The interior is spacious and
comfortable, with long wooden tables.
The outdoor tables enjoy a stunning view.

la Cantina ♥ⅰ☀♥★ ▸B

041 5228258, Cannaregio 3689, Campo San Felice
● 11 am–10 pm, closed Sunday and Monday

A wonderful spot to sit at one of the tables outside and smile at people hurrying back and forth along the Strada Nuova. Savour a glass of draught beer or *prosecco*, or better still choose from one of the more serious bottles that Andrea has on offer. Allow yourself to be tempted by the freshly made snacks.

Have a small roll or *bruschetta* with roast pork, smoked beef, gorgonzola, anchovies, artichokes, olive pâté, dried tomatoes, or quail's eggs and grilled asparagus, *burrata* and aringa sciocca (unsalted herring) or pears with parmesan cheese and *mostarda di cren*. Some say the service is slow and the prices high, but this is the perfect spot for those who want to eat little and well, knowing that the food is freshly made. Regulars perch on the stools at the bar, swapping chit-chat with Francesco, watching him at work and trying to pick up a few tips. There's always a bowl of hot soup at midday, perhaps pasta and beans, pumpkin and smoked speck ham or chickling and emmer.
In season, you'll find day-fresh, hand-harvested oysters and tartufi di mare (*Venus verrucosa* shellfish).

Cantinone storico [€ 47] ✕☀ ▸F

041 5239577, Dorsoduro 660, San Vio, closed Sunday

A classic trattoria with a classic menu in a classic setting. After the wildly imaginative and slightly

disorienting contemporary art in the nearby Guggenheim, it's a relief to sit down to a traditional meal. Warm yourself in winter with a plate of fish soup or enjoy some tagliolini with crab at a table outside in the summer. Prices are honest, which is no small thing.

Cantinone – già Schiavi 🍷🍴 ▶ F

041 5230034, Dorsoduro 992, Ponte San Trovaso ⏺ 8 am–8.30 pm, closed Sunday afternoon

Does anybody still not know about the Cantinone? The walls are completely obscured by bottles, to the delight of browsers enjoying an *ombréta* at the bar. There's a superb selection, from everyday table plonk to wines for great occasions. Ten or so are available by the glass, offering a good opportunity to get to know the wines of the Veneto and perhaps take a bottle home. Try a subtly aromatic Bianco di Custoza, a youthful Soave, an assertive Cabernet from Pramaggiore, a fragrant Sauvignon from the Colli Euganei, a sweet Recioto or a classic *Prosecco* from Valdobbiadene. Nibble a piece of cheese or mortadella and a *crostino* with *baccalà* or leek and tuna, or even tartare sauce and cocoa powder, for the more gastronomically adventurous.

–33

Cavatappi [€ 18/42] ✗🍷🍴 ☀🌙♥★ ▶ D

041 2960252, San Marco 525, Campo della Guerra ⏺ 9 am–12 pm, closed Sunday evening and Monday

A modern, well-lit *enoteca* with food, Cavatappi is a safe haven in the tourist-squeezing centre of the city. There are no traditional *cichèti* but you will find carefully selected cheeses and wines from various regions of Italy. These alternate every two months. Also available are tempting *tramezzini* and *crostini* to go with your glass of wine, chosen from the twenty or so on offer. At midday, there are good rice and pasta dishes (€ 8), such as pumpkin and scampi risotto or spaghettini with fresh tomato and baby squid, but Marco and Francesco can also give you a one-dish meal with vegetables and a glass of wine for € 11. In the evening, there are more elaborate offerings such as swordfish, eggplants and baby tomatoes on a base of potatoes and the extremely popular sliced tuna with balsamic vinegar and baby vegetables.

Cea [€ 28]  ▶ B

041 5237450, Cannaregio 5422a, Campiello Stella
● 9 am–10 pm, closed Saturday evening and Sunday

This is a quiet part of town. At Cea, you can sit under the branches and enjoy an inexpensive meal at an eatery for building workers and cash-strapped youngsters that is also known to one or two *forèsti*.

There are several fixed price options at midday (€ 12-14), such as spaghetti in tomato sauce, fried sardines and *tegolìne* as well as spaghetti with cockles, fried fish, grilled cuttlefish, mixed salads and steaks.

Centrale [€ 80] X ▮ ♀ ◗ ◯ ▶ D

041 2960664, San Marco 1659b, Piscina Frezzeria
● 6.30 pm–2 am, open all week

A "restaurant lounge", as an advertising agent might say, for thirty-somethings who like very low lighting, slouching in a comfortable armchair and sipping something superior. The restaurant is a tad pretentious, and the prices are sometimes over-ambitious, but the kitchen does stay open until late. That makes it the ideal place to come after an evening at the nearby Fenice theatre for a little supper to quell those pangs of night starvation.

al Cicheto ☞ X ♀ ▶ A

041 716037, Cannaregio 367, cCalle della Misericordia
● 7.30 am–7.30 pm, closed Saturday afternoon and Sunday

If you've missed your train, you might want to have something to eat while you wait. Leave the station, stride quickly past the bars, masks and Andean pan pipers, and head down this narrow *calletta* where you will find a quiet eatery frequented only by locals. Enjoy the *polpette, arancini, mozzarella in carrozza* or *tramezzini,* or perhaps sit down to some pasta or rice (€ 4).

alla Ciurma ♥ ☀ ⚲ ▶ B

041 5239514, San Polo 406, Rialto
🕐 7.30 am–7.30 pm, closed Sunday

A recently opened but already very popular *osteria*, particularly at midday. The reasons are the wide range of bar snacks and the friendly staff. There's an impressive display of traditional *cichèti*, and of more creative *crostini*, while if you're looking for a good *ombra* there is an embarrassment of riches.

Corte sconta [€ 52] ✕ ▯ ☀ ★ ▶ E

041 5227024, Castello 3886, Calle del Pestrin, closed Sunday and Monday

The name may recall Italian cartoonist Hugo Pratt but this is a genuinely high-class eatery and one of Venice's hidden gastronomic treasures. Claudio, Lucia and Rita offer sensitively sophisticated reinterpretations of traditional lagoon cuisine. The list of starters is endless: anchovies in marinade, *gransèola* pâté, *schìe* with *polenta*, *latti di seppia*, *garùsoli*, *sardèle in saór*, *canòce* and so on. You can even some of everything in a tasting meal (€ 26). First courses feature day-fresh pasta, *gnocchetti* with *ganasséte* of monkfish and fresh peas or tagliolini with *canòce* and *fondi di carciofo*. Meat and fish courses include grills and mixed fries, *bisàto sull'ara* (eel with bay leaves), baby red mullet with lemon and cardamom, and dory with orange. Round it all off with a traditional *zabaiòn* and Venetian biscuits. The wine list runs to about a hundred labels and there's a good selection of grappas. Pratt's most famous character, Corto Maltese, would be proud!

SARDÈLE FRITE

–35

al Covo [€ 84] ✕ ▮ ☀ ★ ▶ E

041 5223812, Castello 3968, Campiello della Pescaria, closed Wednesday and Thursday

Simply the best. A small, elegant restaurant on Campiello della Pescheria, behind Riva degli Schiavoni, al Covo is a magnet for gourmets from Venice and beyond. Even if you can't tell a cuttlefish from a *folpéto*, you won't be able to resist Cesare's sheer enthusiasm for the flavours of the territory. Listen open-mouthed as he explains the precise difference between fish caught at the harbour mouth and the catch a couple of hundred metres further out. You can look into the kitchen from the dining area but you won't see any tins, animal fats or thickening agents. All you will see is fresh, unfarmed fish that goes into traditional, and sometimes forgotten, recipes sensitively reinterpreted to exalt the freshness of their ingredients. You might try raw fish and shellfish with vegetables, fish soups, *gnocchi* with fillets of *gò*, stewed eel, fried fish and grilled fish. Meat lovers will also find one or two delights, such as the exceptional thin-sliced rump steak. The sweets are also very popular. Don't miss the chocolate cake with dark chocolate sauce. There's also an eight-course tasting menu (€ 75). There are three hundred entries on the wine list, as well as forty spirits and ten olive oils to choose from.

ae Cravate [€ 42] ✎ ♥ ✕ ▶ C

041 5287912, Santa Croce 36, Salizada San Pantalon ◑ 8 am–11 pm, closed Sunday

Two partners, a dash of experience, oodles of enthusiasm and a friend's tie collection led to the opening of this new *osteria con cucina* with a traditional style, plus one or two contributions from Tuscany, courtesy of the chef, Argo. He offers leek soup, lasagne, ribollita (Tuscan vegetable soup), *muséto* and about twenty wines by the glass at the bar, with *polpette*, *paninetti*, baby cuttlefish and so on to nibble at. The dining area can seat about thirty. We'll be keeping an eye on the tie rack.

da Dante ☞ ♥ ☀ ♥ ▶ E

041 5285163, Castello 2877, Corte Nova
🕐 8 am–9 pm, closed Sunday

One of the last surviving genuinely
working-class *osterie*. To get in, you have
to duck under a *sotopòrtego*, and past a shrine to a black Virgin, in the San Lorenzo district of Castello.
Ask for a glass of white or red and a *mèso vòvo*, an *aciugheta*, a cuttlefish, a plate of *bovolèti* in garlic and
parsley, *nervéti*, or perhaps *garùsoli*. Then watch the timeless ritual of the
old men playing cards.

al Diavolo e l'acqua santa [€ 50] ✕ ♥ ▶ B, D

041 2770307, San Polo 561, Rialto 🕐 8 am–9 pm, closed Monday evening and Tuesday

Despite the menu translated into Chinese,
which hints at a certain familiarity with
tourists, this is an *osteria* with all the traditional
trimmings, from *sardèle in saór* to *nervéti* with
onion and *bìgoli in salsa* or with cuttlefish ink.
The atmosphere is lively, noisy and informal
since this is a popular spot with many of the
locals who work in the nearby market. Don't
bother with a table. Enjoy an *ombra* and a plate
of snacks at the bar. Choose from *polpette*, *sépe
róste* (grilled cuttlefish), *testìna* or omelettes.

al Diporto [€ 38] ☞ ✕ ☀ 🐾 ▶ H

041 5285978, Sant'Elena 25, Calle Cengio, closed Monday

You're with a group of friends in the Biennale gardens, and you're looking for something to eat,
perhaps with a glass of cool white wine to wash it down. Look no further. Al Diporto is an unpretentious
trattoria, in the heart of the out-of-the-way Sant'Elena district, and it's always crowded after matches at

the nearby football stadium or on warm
summer's evenings. The cooking is honest
and so are the prices. Try a mixed boiled
seafood *antipasto* of *canòce*, *folpéti* and
shrimp, fried fish and a salad. Make a note
of the address. And after your meal, have a
nice walk back!

Do colonne ☞ ♥ ☀ ✕ ♥ ▸ A

041 5240453, Cannaregio 1814c, Rio Terà San Leonardo
● 10 am–8.30 pm, closed Saturday

It's a relief to find somewhere in the bustling Rio Terà San Leonardo where you can fill that empty corner mid morning, or assuage your lunchtime hunger with a temptingly wide array of nibbles. The huge counter is laden with excellent black bread *tramezzini* with roast pork and mustard or beef and vegetables (€ 2), *mèsi vòvi*, *polpette* (€ 1.30), mini *panini* with cold cuts (€ 1) *crostini* and the odd hot dish (€ 7). Then stagger back to work.

ai Do draghi ☞ ♥ ☀ ✕ ♥ ▸ C, F

041 5289731, Dorsoduro 3665, Campo Santa Margherita
● 7.30 am–10 pm (until 2 am in summer),
closed Thursday (only in winter)

38_ This is the only place in Campo Santa Margherita where you can go not just to have a look around but also to enjoy the good *tramezzini* with smoked speck ham, brie and rocket, or fresh greens and buffalo mozzarella, an excellent *sprìtz*, a glass of draught beer or sample one of the forty wines on offer. The vaguely bistrot-style atmosphere is popular with radicals nostalgic for the Paris of May 1968. Don't be surprised if you find yourself overhearing conversations about books, films or Hegelian hermeneutics at the tables in the *campo*.

Do mori ♥ ▸ B

041 5225401, San Polo 429, Calle dei Do Mori ● 8 am–8.30 pm, closed Sunday

Despite its insistence on including the dreaded crab claws among its *cichèti*, and calling any old fizz *prosecco*, this is still one of the most characteristic stops on a *giro di ombre*. The historically inclined will appreciate that it is one of the oldest *osterie* in the Rialto area, and the hungry will enjoy the

snack counter, which is well-stocked even in mid afternoon. Try a francobollo (a "stamp", or mini *tramezzino*) or a *saltimbocca* in sauce, a *fondo di carciofo* or a tuna *polpetta*, washing it down with an *ombra* of house wine.

ae Do spade [€ 46] ✕♥ ▶B

041 5210583, San Polo 860, Calle Do Spade ● 10 am–3 pm and 6 pm–12 pm, closed Wednesday

If you're looking for an open-minded, informal atmosphere where you can spend a couple of hours in noisy company, then this is the place for you. There are traditional, if unambitious, *cichèti* available at the bar, including *polpette*, *baccalà*, octopus salad and, sadly, crab claws and stuffed Ascoli olives. There's a Venetian menu if you prefer a sit-down meal.

alle Due gondolette [€ 24] 🖝✕♥✳🛴 ▶A

041 717523, Cannaregio 3016, Fondamenta Coletti
● 7 am–2 pm, closed Saturday and Sunday

The name may be stereotypically Venetian but you won't find many tourists here. If you're in the area at midday, make sure you pop in to what is one of the last remaining working-class eateries in the city. Diners can still eat well without breaking the bank, thanks to Davide and his formidable wife Luisa, who offer genuine home-style cooking with a twist of imagination. You might find pasta with Mediterranean-style rabbit sauce, or with an eggplant and pepper pesto, baked lasagne with *radicchio* and artichokes, beef roulade stuffed with mushrooms, roast rabbit or pork, chicken balls, meat loaf with pumpkin. Cooked and fresh vegetables are a staple on the menu. The dining room opens in the evening for small groups if you book in advance.

al Faro [€ 32] 🖝✕✳🛴 ▶A

041 2750794, Cannaregio 1181, Gheto Vechio, closed Tuesday

Let's try to get things straight. The management here is Brazilian-Jordanian and the cook is from Bengal. The menu features pizzas, Thai fish and a few attractive made-to-order specialties like rice with shrimp and vegetables or exotic *gnocchi* with vegetables, avocado and mozzarella. You might be feeling a little confused when you get up from your table outdoors, especially when you realise you are in the heart of the Jewish quarter, the Ghetto. This is one of those addresses that come in handy when you're looking for somewhere pleasant and not too budget-stretching.

TAGLIOLINI
NERI CON RAGÙ
DI ASTICE

Fiaschetteria toscana [€ 70] ✗ ⬤ ☀ ★ ▶ B

041 5285281, Cannaregio 5719, Salizada San Giovanni Grisostomo, closed Tuesday and Wednesday morning

The refined, unfussy atmosphere provides the setting for a wide-ranging menu featuring the great creations of the Veneto kitchen. Meat and fish dishes are prepared with first-quality ingredients that follow the changing seasons. Enjoy *gransèola*, *schìe* with *polenta*, *risotto di gò e bevaràsse* or black tagliolini with lobster sauce.

The mixed fry of monkfish, squid, *moéche* (soft-shell crab) and cuttlefish is to die for and the down-to-earth Mariuccia is as memorable as her sweets, such as honey and hazelnut parfait with chocolate sauce or caramel apple turnover with ice cream.

The cellar is Albino's little indulgence. He has more than nine hundred wines! If you want to order a particular bottle, you'll have to argue with Roberto, Claudio and Lollo, who have ideas of their own. There is a select trolley of small-production raw milk and seasonal cheeses. During the week, the restaurant offers an attractively priced (€ 20) midday menu.

Fiore ❦ ▶ D, F

041 5235310, San Marco 3461, Calle de le Botteghe
⊙ 9 am–10.30 pm, closed Tuesday

Fiore is an *osteria*-trattoria, not to be confused with Da Fiore, which is in a completely different location – and price band. The restaurant is a bit touristy so head straight for the busy bar, where you will find *polpettine*, *nervéti* with onion, *folpéti* with celery, *lugànega* and many other tempting *cichèti*.

If the *sprìtz* has gone to your head, you can sit down in the *calle*.

da Fiore [€ 120] ✕ 🍶 ★ ▶ C

041 721308, San Polo 2202a, Calle del
Scaleter, closed Sunday and Monday

One of Venice's most exclusive
restaurants, Da Fiore is in
the top bracket for price and
for the quality of the cuisine.
Its discreetly elegant art deco
interior, the great and the good
who dine here and above all

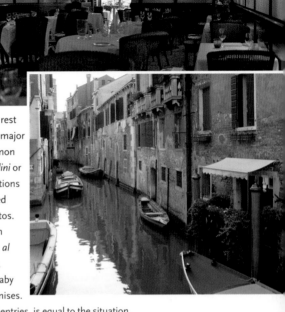

the je ne sais quoi that sets it apart from the rest
ensure Da Fiore a prominent place in all the major
guides. Starters to try include scampi or salmon
in marinade, *canòce*, *garùsoli*, boiled *moscardini* or
schìe with soft *polenta*. The list of *primi* – portions
are particularly generous for such a renowned
establishment – features tempting fish risottos.
Among the *secondi* you'll find baked turbot in
a crust of potatoes, *branzino* with vegetables *al
cartoccio* and, depending on the time of year,
mixed fries of *canestrèi*, *moéche*, scampi or baby
squid. The desserts are all made on the premises.
Naturally, the wine list, with its five hundred entries, is equal to the situation.
Service can be a little stiff-backed and unless you get a substantial discount, prices are stiff, too.
And perhaps just a little over-ambitious.

Fontana [€ 35] 🐾 ✕ ☀ ▶ A

041 715077, Cannaregio 1102, Fondamenta di Cannaregio ● 7 pm–10 pm, closed Sunday

Swept by the north lagoon winds, between the Ponte delle Guglie and the Ghetto, is a long-established
osteria that sells unbottled Veneto and Friulian wines to a working-class clientele.
For the past few years, it has also been a small, well-run trattoria with a homely atmosphere.
Try the spaghetti with eel, *gransèola* risotto or *gnocchi* with turbot
and courgettes. The indoor dining room is comfortable and the
tables on the *fondamenta* are delightful.

al Fontego dei pescaori [€ 47]
X ✦ ☀★ ▶ B

041 5200538, Cannaregio 3711, Sotoportego del Tagiapiera, closed Tuesday

Bare brick walls, wooden furniture, a warm, welcoming atmosphere and carefully laid tables set the tone in this spacious former residence and warehouse with its characteristic portico on the canal and small courtyard to the rear.

Fish dominates the menu, here and there with an oriental flavour or dressed with aromatic herbs. Accompanying it are estuary-grown vegetables – shrimp and artichoke salad, *gransèola* and asparagus tips, tagliolini with wild asparagus and *bevaràsse* – but there is also room on the menu for meat, such as tagliata (thin slices) of beef, lamb chops or stuffed duck in *peverada* sauce. There's an excellent list of wines, many available by the glass.

Frary's bar [€ 22] ☞ X ▼ ▶ C

041 720050, San Polo 2559, Fondamenta dei Frari ● 11 am–3 pm and 6 pm–11 pm, closed Tuesday

This down-to-earth eatery is a pot pourri of Mediterranean and Middle Eastern cooking, mixing Greek, Lebanese, Bedouin, Kurdish and Tunisian styles. Its selling points include Luca's seraphic calm and the very affordable prices. The menu features falafel (fried chickpea balls), dolmades (rice wrapped in vine leaves), tzaziki, hummus, souvlaki (spicy chicken on a skewer), kubbe (Kurdish rice balls with spiced meat), mansaf (Bedouin rice with chicken, almonds and yoghurt), couscous vegetarian style, or with mutton, chicken or seafood (shrimp, octopus and squid), and magluba (rice, vegetables, chicken, sultanas, pine nuts, yoghurt and mint). The pistachio, date, raisin and rosewater ice cream is mouth-watering.

There's a short € 10 menu at midday.

SPANAKOPITA

KEFTES

VERDURE CON FORMAGGIO HALLUMI

SOUVLAKI

FALAFEL

KUBBE

alla Frasca [€ 18/50] ✕❦☀⚔ ▶B

041 5285433, Cannaregio 5176, Campiello della Carità ☻ 11 am–3 pm and 6.30 pm–11 pm, closed Tuesday evening

This small, picturesque *osteria* is in a lovely *campiello*, tucked away in the maze of *calli* and *callette* near Fondamente Nove. The pasta is made on the premises, and there are some traditional fish dishes, but the aroma of lamb chops and other fragrances tell you the owner is from Abruzzo.

At midday, there's a tempting, very affordable menu at € 12 for local workers and anyone else who drops in.

−43

Ganesh Ji [€ 32] ✕☀ ▶C

041 719804, San Polo 2426, Rio Marin, closed Wednesday and Thursday morning

The colourful Patrizia deftly runs this Indian restaurant with Indian cooks who, thankfully, dose the spices for Venetian palates. People come here for the inexpensive prices, vegetarian dishes and tandoori cooking.
If you fancy a taste of the Orient, try the chicken shai and chicken nuggets in a delicate yoghurt, saffron, almond, cashew and spice sauce.
Takeaway service available.

al Garanghélo (1) [€ 32] 🖙✕❦☀♥ ▶B

041 721721, San Polo 1570, Calle dei Botteri ☻ 8 am–10 pm, closed Sunday

Expert, polite and very likeable. That sums up Renzo in the kitchen and Annalisa at the bar, the two well-matched partners who run this popular *osteria con cucina*, dominated by its counter groaning under *cichèti* and house specialties. You can let yourself be tempted to sit down by the

smiling hospitality, a rare treat in a city of generally grumpy restaurateurs. Enjoy an evening meal, perhaps starting with some pasta made on the premises and finishing off with a luscious budino del doge dessert. This is a place for regulars and the occasional curious tourist, who will quickly be adopted and given affectionate, helpful advice.

al Garanghélo (2) [€ 48] ✕ ♥ ☀ ▶ E

041 5204967, Castello 1621, Via Garibaldi
🕐 10 am–3 pm and 6 pm–10 pm, closed Tuesday

A trattoria with a well-stocked *cichèto* counter and a traditional menu, including *sardèle in saór*, seafood salad, *baccalà* in various styles and grilled scampi. It's a noisy, fun place, especially in the evenings when local singer Lucio Bisutto turns up. He's the brother of Simone, the landlord, and owner of the restaurant next door, who turns the dining area into a... *garanghélo*.

da Gino ☞ ♥ ☀ ✕ ▶ F

041 5285276, Dorsoduro 853a, Calle Nova Sant'Agnese
🕐 6 am–7.30 pm, closed Sunday

Signor Emilio at the espresso machine means that this is the place to come for the best cup of coffee in Dorsoduro. Most of Emilio's family work behind the counter or serve at table, ensuring that the atmosphere is relaxed and easygoing. Students love this bar, which has enough space for you to be sure of finding somewhere to sit down with your *panino*.

Gislon [€ 34] ☞ ✕ ♥ ▶ B, D

041 5223569, San Marco 5424a, Calle della Bissa 🕐 9 am–9.30 pm, open all week

In the heart of Venice at San Bartolomeo, a stone's throw from Rialto and not much further from St Mark's Square, here is your chance to try all Venice's culinary delights – and one or two others – at helpfully economical prices. Set aside your first impression of a tourist trap and take a good look at

the long counter. You'll see meat, fish or vegetable *pasticcio*, soups, risottos, octopus salad, boiled vegetables, *baccalà mantecato* or *alla vicentina*, veal stew and *cotolotte alla milanese*.

This is the ideal spot for a quick lunchtime snack propped against one of the high shelves or sitting down at a table on the upper floor.

When you have elbowed your way to the bar, you can sample the *mozzarella in carrozza* with anchovies or ham, and the *arancini di riso*.

ai Gondolieri [€ 86] ✕ ▶ F

041 5286396, Dorsoduro 336,
Ponte del Formager, closed Tuesday

An only apparently modest
eatery that actually offers
many refined surprises. It's
very near the Guggenheim,
where Giovanni also runs the museum's coffee shop.

The meat and vegetable-based menu includes terrine of white meat, fat and preserves, oven-baked
s'ciòsi in their shells, tepid salad of venison with blueberries, panzerotti pasta envelopes filled with
Jerusalem artichokes and Montasio cheese fondue, pappardelle pasta with lamb and late *radicchio*
sauce, fillet of Argentine Angus beef with juniper berries or saddle of lamb with Barolo and *radicchio*.
In autumn, truffles dominate the menu and prices rise in proportion. The desserts and cheese trolley
will satisfy the most discriminating palates. Nor will the wine list disappoint.

Harry's bar [€ 210] ✕ ▼ ▶ D

041 5285777, San Marco 1323, Calle Vallaresso ● 10.30 am–11 pm, open all week

Harry's is still a classic. Its lustre may have dulled slightly, but it continues to haul in awards and
mentions in all the right places.

Genuinely, budget-shatteringly expensive, Harry's has what we might call a personal pricing policy that
enables it to hold on to a hard core of Venetian customers, including lawyers, university professors and
more or less distinguished members of the local aristocracy.

The tactic means that Harry's is not one of those places for
well-heeled *forèsti*. People come here to be part of the world of
international celebrities, or rather to show everyone that they can
get within shoulder-rubbing distance of them.

Some of the items on the menu are still incomparably good, such
as the risotto primavera, the oven-baked white tagliolini with ham,
the *carpaccio* and the curried dory with pilaf rice.

Portions, and the quantity of butter used, come from another
age and one course is often enough.

If all this is beyond your budget, then at least indulge in a cocktail
at the bar. Sip a Bellini (€ 14) or a Martini on one of Harry's
high stools, perhaps with a pierino (small, almost fried, toasted
sandwiches) or two. You can then wander off to an *osteria* and
spend the evening telling everyone how much taller George
Clooney looks on television.

da Ignazio [€ 47] ✗♈♙☀♟ ▶C

041 5234852, San Polo 2749, Calle dei Saoneri, closed Saturday

After picking your way through a bewildering maze of dark, narrow *calli*, you will emerge into a bright, spacious courtyard where, weather permitting, you can enjoy your meal under an attractive pergola.

Venetians are very fond of this eatery, partly because of the informal yet faultless service and partly because the menu is solidly traditional. Prominently featured are fan shell scallops, *canòce*, *gransèole*, risottos and lots of excellent fish, whether baked, fried or above all grilled. There's a wine list and a good selection of grappas and whiskies. Popular among family groups with grandparents in tow.

da Lele ☞♈ ▶C

Santa Croce 183, Campo dei Tolentini ⊙ 6 am–2 pm and 4 pm–8 pm, closed Saturday afternoon and Sunday

Little more than a hole in the wall, da Lele is a Venetian institution, especially for commuters and teachers, students and office staff at the nearby faculty of architecture, who drop in for a cheering glass of Merlot, Cabernet or Raboso (€ 0.80). Genuine *clintòn* arrives in November, and soon runs out. The small *panini* (€ 0.80) are fantastic. Try *pancetta* and small artichokes, spicy salami and Asiago mezzano cheese, lard from Valle d'Aosta (we are heartily fed up with Colonna clones), local garlic salami, roast pork or mortadella. You'll often find Fabio, the owner's son, serving. He is gradually taking over the running of this unique corner of Venice.

Leon bianco 🐾✕🍷 ▶D

041 5221180, San Marco 4153, Salizada San Luca
● 8 am–6 pm, closed Saturday and Sunday

A bar-cum-*osteria* where friendly
staff serve hot filling food at
affordable prices (€ 4-6), such as
pasta in tomato sauce, lasagne with
Bolognese sauce, *rìsi e bìsi*, roast
meat and potatoes or cuttlefish and

polenta. But equally meticulous care goes into the preparation of the enticing toasted sandwiches.
In short, this is a good place to come for an inexpensive midday snack.

Linea d'ombra [€ 60] 🍷✕☀ ▶G

041 2411881, Dorsoduro 19, Ponte dell'Umiltà ● 9 am–11 pm, closed Wednesday

The location is spectacular, as is the waterside terrace with its superb
view ranging from the mainland along the whole of the Giudecca to
San Giorgio. Indoors, the dining area is elegantly
modern and beautifully accessoried. In line with
Linea d'ombra's high standards, the offerings on
the menu have names that spill over onto two lines
and could perhaps do with a little editing.
But this is still an excellent place for an aperitif or a
long drink before you stroll along a stretch of front
that has always been a firm favourite with couples
in love.

–47

alla Madonna [€ 44] 🖙 X ▶ B, D

041 5223824, San Polo 594, Calle de la Madonna, closed Wednesday

A very large restaurant near Rialto, alla Madonna
is tried, trusted and well loved. Commodious and
always crowded, the dining area caters for hordes of
hungry clients while maintaining good levels of service
– white tablecloths and fast, attentive waiters – as well
as equally good food. The high turnover means the
kitchen can offer quality and an extensive menu of fish

and meat dishes at prices that are hard to find anywhere else. On the menu
are *sarde in saór*, *gransèola*, *folpéti*, fish soup, *schìe*, eels, fried squid, cuttlefish,
grilled red mullet and lobster with mayonnaise, as well as lasagne *pasticcio*, tripe,
Venetian-style liver, roast chicken, *cotoletta alla milanese*, grilled veal chops and
more, all accompanied by seasonal vegetables. It's the perfect spot for a large
family gathering when you know that everyone will want something different. No
bookings are taken but you don't usually have to wait long for a table.

Marcà 🖙 ♈ ☀ ▶ B

347 1002583, San Polo 213, Campo Bella Vienna
● 9 am–3 pm and 6 pm–9.30 pm, closed Sunday

A favourite rendezvous for students
and professionals for its strategic
location and swift service.
If you want somewhere to sit down, look
elsewhere. There's barely room for the
counter and a bench outside. But you also
have the entire *campo* at your disposal if you
want to stop passing friends and chat with
a glass in your hand. Around twenty more
than decent wines by the glass accompany
tempting *panini* with sfilacci di cavallo
(shredded horsemeat), artichokes and
robiola cheese or tuna, celery and olives,
or simply with excellent cold cuts. If you
prefer, try the meat or vegetable *polpette*.

da Mario [€ 35] ✕ ▶ D

041 5285968, San Marco 2614, Fondamenta de la Malvasia Vecia, open all week

Se magna ben co' pochi schei (You eat well for not much money) is how Signora Annalisa sums up her trattoria. And there could be no crisper description of this unfussy eatery that looks as if it was put into a deep freeze in the 1950s and defrosted just the other day. In this very central but secluded location, you'll be able to savour a thoroughly Venetian menu of meat and fish dishes at very affordable prices.

dalla Marisa [€ 27 carne/36 pesce] ☞ ✕ ☀ ♥ ▶ A

041 720211, Cannaregio 652b, Fondamenta San Giobbe, closed Sunday, Monday and Wednesday evenings

If you're not from Venice, bring a dictionary – and that goes for Italian speakers, too. This is the most Venetian eatery in the city, even though it has recently been discovered by *forèsti* and features in many of the guidebooks. But Marisa hasn't changed and continues to do what she has always done. The scion of a long line of *bechèri*, or butchers, she offers genuine cooking that predictably puts the accent on meat. Duck sauces grace huge plates of tagliatelle, there are risottos with *sècoe*, *sguassétti alla bechéra* (beef in gravy), mixed boiled meats, tripe and succulent venison ragouts with seasonal vegetables.

–49

Everything is absolutely fresh and cooked to order. At the end of your meal, you'll be given the traditional doggie bag with your leftovers. Intimacy is not a strong point, so we recommend it for small groups rather than a one-on-one dinner. When you book, which is practically mandatory, you'll be told whether the menu will be meat, game or fish-based.

alla Mascareta [€ 50] ✕ ▼ ♦ ★ ▶ B, D, E

041 5230744, Castello 5183, Calle Lunga Santa Maria Formosa
◉ 7 pm–2 am, closed Wednesday and Thursday

This is the realm of Mauro Lorenzon, wielder of sabres, devourer of oysters, connoisseur of champagnes, president of Enoiteche (you'll have to ask him what it means), theorist of unfiltered wines and much, much more. The creations of his kitchen are at your disposal until the wee small hours. Select from crêpes with asparagus and scallops, stuffed quail, Alpago lamb, refined cheese and cold cut boards, *crostini* and after dinner a sweet wine with petit fours, a glass of fine champagne or a grappa selected from the range on offer. Without question, one of Venice's most comfortable *enoteche* with a bar area for wines by the glass and a quiet, welcoming dining room furnished with lovely tables and old wooden dressers. Just outside, cinema-style seats against the window provide somewhere to sit in the *calle*.
If you want to take home a little treat, the *enoteca* shop opposite has bottles, sauces, preserves, vinegars and oils.

al Mascaron [€ 55] ✕ ▶ B, D, E

041 5225995, Castello 5225, Calle Lunga Santa Maria Formosa, closed Sunday

Venetians will tell you "it isn't what it used to be". But what is? The tables are jammed closer together, they don't serve wine by the glass at the bar and the prices are no longer all that attractive, but al Mascaron is still a paradigm for traditional *osterie* with its wooden tables, paper napkins from an economy pack, typical atmosphere, mixed *antipasti* – *latti di seppia*, marinaded anchovies, octopus salads, *baccalà mantecato* and grilled cuttlefish – and huge plates of spaghetti with lobster or cockles.

SPAGHETTI CON L'ASTICE

NIGHIRI

URAMAKI

HOSOMAKI

GARI

WASABI

Mirai [€ 60] ✗ ☀ ★ ▶ A

041 2206517, Cannaregio 227, Lista di Spagna, open evenings only, closed Monday

Venice's only Japanese restaurant – but it's a good one – is at the
Hotel Amadeus, where it takes advantage of the lovely indoor garden
with candles, cushions, low tables and an Oriental atmosphere.
Do try the raw fish sashimi, which here is usually salmon, tuna or bass
served with soya sauce and wasabi, the hot Japanese green horseradish,
onigiri (rice balls with a piece of raw fish), uramaki (rice rolled around
fish) and hosomaki (thin sushi rolls) washed down with sake or Japanese
beer. If you are on your own, or just with a friend, sit at the counter and watch
how Akira prepares the food. Watch what you say, though. Akira can give you a piece
of his mind in fluent Venetian! Hadakaimasu (enjoy your meal). Kampai (cheers).

_51

Mistrà [€ 48] ✗ ▶ G

041 5220743, Giudecca 212a, Consorzio Cantieristica Minore area, closed Monday evening and Tuesday

Disembark at the Redentore, turn your back on the city and head into an area of small boatyards where
you can admire the magical lights of the entire south lagoon. On the first floor of a former boatyard
building – reached by a panoramic outside staircase – you'll find a well-lit restaurant run by Roberta
and Alessandro. The cooking is a bit Ligurian and a bit

Venetian, with pasta or rice in fresh fish and shellfish
sauces then octopus salad with potatoes, baby squid
soup, trofie pasta with pesto sauce, spaghetti *al
cartoccio*, and salt-baked, grilled or baked fish.
At midday, there's a € 12
menu for workers from the
boatyards in the area.

Monaco – Gran canal [€ 85] ✗ ▼ ☀ ▶ D

041 5200211, San Marco 1332, Calle Vallaresso ☉ 10 am–12 pm, open all week

If you enjoy being cosseted and feeling special, this famous restaurant adjoining the hotel of the same name might be the just place for you. The magnificent terrace looks onto the point of Santa Maria della Salute,

where the Grand Canal opens into the shimmering Bacino di San Marco. The view is unique and the service impeccable. The setting makes the brief menu look equally exceptional, even though it lacks peaks of sensory excellence or any especially

sophisticated creations. We suggest the salmon and swordfish tartare, tagliolini with scampi, grilled fish or beef and, to round off the meal, apple tatin (upside-down tart) or an amaretto dessert. Popular with tourists and more affluent local residents.

un Mondo divino ▼ ▲ ♥ ★ ▶ B

041 5211093, Cannaregio 5984a, Salizada San Canciano
☉ 10 am–3 pm and 5.30 pm–9.30 pm, closed Monday

What a fantastic discovery! Here are some of the secrets behind the success of Cora and Raffaele, as likeable a couple as they are good-looking, not to say scrupulous about the freshness of the products on their specialty-packed counter. They have *polpettine* in sauce, oven-baked mussels, *nervéti*, oysters on Friday, barely marinaded

bass and salmon or raw tartufi di mare (*Venus verrucosa* shellfish). About forty wines are available by the glass. There's a wooden counter, tall stools and shelves to lean and snack on. Service is informal and very attentive. Very well done indeed!

los Murales [€ 15/30] ✕ ☀ 🐟 ▶ G

041 5230004, Giudecca 70, Fondamenta Zitelle
closed Wednesday in summer, Sunday in winter

Disembark at the Zitelle and there you are. This
is the least expensive spot in the city and the one
with the most stunning view. Popular with locals,
including family groups, but patronised mainly by
youngsters in small boats kitted out with ghetto
blasters. At midday the menu is based on meat
(€ 11) or fish (€ 15). In the evening, the cuisine
turns Mexican, believe it or not, with maize tortillas, vegetables, cheese, beans beef and chicken.
Try the arroz valenciana (rice casserole), burritos, tacos or fajitas, then finish with a crema catalana.

Muro [€ 35/52] ✕ 🍸♥ ▶ B

041 5237495, San Polo 222, Campo Bella Vienna ⏰ 8 am–3 pm and 5 pm–1 am, closed Sunday

Very popular at the cocktail hour, and also after dinner. Young architects, lawyers and lots
of people-who-know-people spill over into the *campo* and sip a *spritz* as they chat at the tables.
Upstairs, wide windows overlook the *campo*. This is the domain of Beppe, a big, muscular Bavarian
with an obviously athletic past who now devotes his attention to the kitchen. During the day, you might
bump into him selecting ingredients at the Rialto market. In the evening, he'll be busy preparing a
range of eclectic if occasionally puzzling dishes. You might find smoked sturgeon salad with courgettes,
coriander and mint, saffron penne pasta with monkfish and liquorice, purple potato soup with herring

–53

tartare or bass with potato strudel
and cherry tomato preserve.
The menu is shorter and less
expensive at midday.
At lunchtime on Saturdays
during the market, you can enjoy
a plate of something in the
campo for a few euros.

Naranzaria ♥️♦♥★ ▶ B, D

041 7241035, San Polo 130, Erbaria di Rialto ● 11 am–3 pm
and 6 pm–1 am (open all day in summer) closed Monday

If you want a midday meal, aperitif, dinner or after-
dinner gathering in very aristocratic surroundings,
this is the place for you. The wines are from
Brandino Brandolini, who is a partner in the
business, and other excellent producers, mainly
Friulian. A few sips as you sit at your table will make
the view over the Erbaria, right on the Grand Canal,
look even more magnificent. Stefano is the other

partner, the one who does all the work. At any time of night
or day, he can serve you a selection of tempting Friulian cold
cuts or something from the ten or so hot dishes (€ 10-15) that
might include *polenta* and shin of beef, *radicchio di Treviso e
pancetta* or soup, as well as light salads or a taboule of shrimp
for any passing models who have to stay in shape.
Thanks to Akira, lovers of sashimi and the like are well catered
for. There's always a good Soave to wash it down.

ARANCIA, FINOCCHIO E OL

ai Nomboli ♥☀️🐿️ ▶ C

041 5230995, San Polo 2717c, Rio Terà dei Nomboli ● 7 am–9 pm, closed Saturday and Sunday

A spot much loved for Mirella's suave courtesy and the quality of Francesco's *tramezzini* and filled

rolls. There is an amazing range, including
asparagus, grilled *radicchio*, roast pork,
gorgonzola, *casatella*, *fondi di carciofo*, nettle
sauce, roast beef, Calabrian *coppa* sausage,
aubergines in oil, *porcini* and of course cold
cuts, from *soprèssa* to smoked speck ham.
There really is something for everyone.
With a little bit of luck, in summertime you
might find a free corner at one of the outdoor
tables where you can watch the comings and
goings between San Polo and San Tomà.

al Nono risorto [€ 38] X🏃☀ ▶ B

041 5241169, Santa Croce 2337, Sottoportego de la Siora Bettina, closed Wednesday and Thursday morning

The young and very informal management of this capacious, vaguely radical spot offers good prices and an opportunity to eat until late.

The ingredients that make this pizza restaurant and trattoria so popular with groups of Venetian thirty-somethings include the big gravel-strewn garden, where in summer you can eat under the wisteria. Good pizzas (from € 5-9), salads and a Venetian menu.

At the entrance, there's a notice board with all the campaigns currently being supported by the management, especially the protest at the Mose barrier system and dirty *calli*.

Oniga [€ 43] X ☀ ▶ F

041 5224410 (347 3216028), Dorsoduro 2852, Campo San Barnaba, closed Tuesday

Don't be surprised if you find goulash on the menu at this friendly, well-lit *enoteca*. Annika in the kitchen is clearly Hungarian and her influence on the menu is evident. But she also serves up much more Venetian dishes, like grilled fish, sautéed mussels, white asparagus with boiled eggs or cockles with garlic *crostini* and other offerings. She does nice pasta and rice dishes with vegetables and shellfish, such as pumpkin

gnocchi with prawns and baby broccoli, or spaghettini with swordfish and cream of pumpkin, as well as spaghetti alla chitarra with veal and chicken sauce, Aberdeen Angus fillet steak and thin sliced tuna with aubergines. Marino will help you select a wine to sip at the open-air tables in Campo San Barnaba.

ai Osti [€ 30] 🗺 ✕ ♥ ☀ ▶ B

041 5207993, Cannaregio 3849, Corte dei Pali
● 10 am–11 pm, closed Sunday

Young Diego has managed to raise
this cramped *osteria* from the ashes
with his marvellous counter of
delicacies, including grilled prawns,
fried fish, *nervéti*, *figà a la venexiana*,
polpettine, vegetables and his trademark *baccalà mantecato*. At midday, there's an inexpensive menu
for the working population and one or two dishes made to order. Booking required in the evening.

alla Palanca [€ 34] 🗺 ✕ ♥ ☀ ▶ G

041 5287719, Giudecca 448, Fondamenta del Ponte Picolo ● 7 am–8.30 pm, closed Sunday

Many of the spots on the Giudecca offer low prices and great views. This bar-trattoria
is a fine example. From the tables on the *fondamenta*, you can enjoy the view over the
whole length of Riva delle Zattere and even a little further on. At midday, there's a € 12
workers' menu or a highly recommended, more sophisticated short menu, again at

reasonable prices, including
swordfish marinaded in
citrus fruits, tagliatelle with
porcini, risotto in cuttlefish
ink and a chocolate mousse
to finish off. Great hospitality
and efficient service. It's
a shame that alla Palanca
doesn't open in the evening.

Pane, vino e San Daniele [€ 40] 🔍 ✕ ♥ ☀ 🐾 ▶ F

041 5237456, Dorsoduro 1722, Campo dell'Anzolo Raffaele ● 10 am–12 pm, closed Wednesday

In the glorious 1960s, this was the *osteria* of the great artists attracted by characterful, out-of-the-
way bars with tables in the *campo*. Today, it is still a lovely place to meet, as researchers from nearby
university departments have discovered. There are Friulian wines, cheese and cold cuts, not to mention
other delights like bread *gnocchi*, San Daniele air-cured ham and crispy frico, Friuli's fried cheese
specialty. As you glance through the menu, items like malloreddu (pasta *gnocchi*)
and rabbit with myrtle could lead you to suspect that the cook is from Sardinia.
You'd be right. At midday, you'll find *mozzarella in carrozza* and the like.

SALSICCE
FRIULAN
E FAVE

da Pinto [€ 36] X ♀ ☀ ▶ B

041 5224599, San Polo 367,
Campo de le Becarie
◉ 10 am–10 pm, closed Monday

Da Pinto was one of Rialto's
oldest *osterie*, a *bàcaro*
selling wine from Puglia
since 1890, and used to
cater for the fish market.

Sadly, the tables indoors and in the *campo* are increasingly monopolised by tourists who have inevitably influenced the food, which now includes lasagne, pizza and cannelloni. Go straight to the bar, where you can console yourself with an *ombra* and some *folpéto rósto* or a *crostino* with *baccalà*. These continue to be good. A new room has significantly expanded the indoor dining area.

al Ponte 👉 ♀ ▶ B

041 5286157, Cannaregio 6378, Ponte del Cavallo
◉ 8 am–9 pm, closed Sunday afternoon

There are plenty of bars in this *calle* but al Ponte has much the most characteristic ambience. You'll find the odd table where you can enjoy a *cichèto* with the approachable, mainly elderly, customers and the odd tourist. There are small *panini* and *crostini* with pancetta steccata (pork belly matured between two pieces of wood), salami, beef and peppers, mortadella, *baccalà mantecato*, one or two salads and the inevitable *ombra*. If you overdo things, the hospital is nearby.

Pontini – da Giada e Roberta [€ 25]
👉 X ♀ ☀ ▶ A

041 714123, Cannaregio 1268, Ponte delle Guglie
◉ 6.30 am–10.30 pm, closed Sunday

A non-stop bar and trattoria that stays open from breakfast to midday meal, afternoon snack, aperitif and evening meal, serving everyone promptly and with courtesy. Locals love it but passing holidaymakers will also drop in. For lunch you'll find spaghetti allo scoglio (spaghetti with seafood sauce), fried fish and *baccalà*.

al Portego [€ 34] 🔍✕🍷 ▶B, D

041 5229038, Castello 6015, Calle de la Malvasia
● 11 am–3 pm and 7 pm–10 pm, closed Sunday

Near a *pòrtego* tucked away between San Lio and Santa Marina
is an *osteria* that is very popular with vaguely radical youngsters.
The reasons are the moderate prices and the vast range of *cichèti*,
including various *crostini*, one or two fried items, *baccalà* and baby
cuttlefish. Not all the offerings are to be recommended – working
mothers aren't the only ones to have discovered frozen food.
There are tables inside for those who want to sit down to a hot dish
of *bìgoli in salsa*, fish risotto, *pasta e fasiòi* or *muséto* and *polenta*.

58_ al Prosecco 🍷🍴☀♥★ ▶C

041 5240222, Santa Croce 1503, Campo San Giacomo dall'Orio ● 8 am–8 pm (till 10.30 pm in summer), closed Sunday

San Giacomo dall'Orio is a serenely quiet *campo* for families, children and dogs. There are even one or
two trees. It's a genuine pleasure to sit here at peace with the world, sipping a good wine professionally
recommended by the reliable staff. These are some of the reasons why more and more Venetians are
leaving their usual beaten track to pop into to this *enoteca* with its smart young managers. Brothers
Stefano and Davide offer a fine selection of cheeses and cold cuts, salads and hot *crostini*. Ten or so
wines are sold by the glass on a rotating basis, and the many bottles can be opened even if it's just for

a single glass. Often, you can enjoy
oysters and raw fish. In winter, the
cosy, comfortable inside room is the
ideal place to read, even if the book
turns out to be a bit boring.

ai Quaranta ladroni [€ 38] ✗❦☀ ▶A

041 715736, Cannaregio 3253, Fondamenta della Sensa ● 10 am–3 pm and 7 pm–11 pm, closed Monday

In the early days, people came here when they couldn't get a table at the Anice stellato next door. Then ai Quaranta ladroni acquired its own reputation and started to gain a following. The food is traditional, but well made. Tried the mixed fish *antipasto* and the *gnocchi alla gransèola*.

Quatro feri [€ 38] ✗♥ ▶F

041 5206978, Dorsoduro 2754a, Calle Lunga San Barnaba, closed Sunday

At the start of the *calle* that goes from Campo San Barnaba towards San Sebastiano stands Quatro feri, the *osteria* in the charge of Barbara, Betty and Davide. It's the perfect place to loosen your belt and get stuck into a generous helping of spaghetti in a delicious seafood sauce, *alla bùsara* or with cockles. Or you could opt for a nice plate of pumpkin *gnocchi* with scallops and *porcini* mushrooms. Before you sit down to the serious stuff, you can nibble at a plate of titbits from the counter, such as octopus and squid salad, *folpéti*, *baccalà mantecato* and lots of vegetables. If you don't want to splash out on a big-name bottle, the house wine is rather good. The atmosphere is more relaxed in the middle of the day.

SPAGHETTI CON
PESCE SPADA,
CREMA DI
MELANZANE E
POMODORI SECCHI

il Refolo [€ 48] ✕ ▮ ☀ ✈ ▶ C

041 5240016, Santa Croce 1459, Campiello del Piovan, closed
Monday and Tuesday morning (open from April to October only)

Eateries don't come much more romantic.
The bridge, the canal, the fountain, the
portico, the church and all the rest add up
to one of Venice's most picturesque corners.
Since this is a fashionable place to eat, you
are sometimes disturbed by noisy water taxis
unloading a celeb who can't be bothered
to walk. Those who make their entrance in
an oared vessel are much more welcome.
If you don't want one of the good, albeit
somewhat expensive, pizzas (€ 7-14),
try a plate of pasta or rice, or perhaps curried
chicken, lamb chops or thin-sliced Irish
Aberdeen Angus. There are some nice beers
available on draught and a short list
of seriously good wines.

Rioba [€ 45] ✕ ▮ ☀ ▶ B

041 5244379, Cannaregio 2553,
Fondamenta de la Misericordia, closed Monday

Bare brick walls, wooden beams and plain tables greet you in this recently opened *osteria*. Well-lit and welcoming, it is named after Rioba, one of the four Moorish merchants, the curiously beturbaned eponymous marble figures in the nearby *campo*. There's a seasonal menu of fish and vegetables with one or two variations, like aubergine pasta envelopes, baked fillet of monkfish with nuts and cherry tomatoes, fillet of *branzino* with *finferli*, *chiodini* and scampi, as well as meat dishes like thin-sliced Aberdeen Angus or breast of duck. In summer, you can sit at one of the many tables on the *fondamenta* or in the *calle*.

Rivetta ☞ ♈♥ ▶ C

Santa Croce 637a, Calle Sechera ● 8.30 am–9.30 pm, closed Sunday

Wine here is served from a demijohn and there are *crostini* with *baccalà* or gorgonzola, *paninetti* with *soppressa*, salami, *pancetta* or grilled aubergines and courgettes, and salads. A never-ending stream of banter between landlord and the drinking public that stops by on the daily *giro di ombre* makes Rivetta a genuine neighbourhood *bàcaro*, not far from the Tolentini church and the railway station.

VOVI DURI
(BOILED EGGS)

Ruga Rialto [€ 37]
☞ ✗ ♈ ☀ ❋ ▶ B, D

041 5211243, San Polo 692, Ruga Rialto
● 11 am–3 pm and 6 pm–12 pm, open all week

A capacious *osteria* for large, noisy groups. There are a few *cichèti* at the bar – *sépe róste*, fried squid or *crostini* – and a short unambitious menu of inexpensive traditional food. The main reason for coming is the simpatia of the three young *osti*, Marco, Giorgio and Giorgio. The trio love to organise themed evenings and on Fridays there is live music.

ai Rusteghi ♈♦ ❋❋ ★ ▶ B, D

041 5232205, San Marco 5513, Corte del Tentor ● 10 am–3 pm and 6 pm–9.30 pm, closed Saturday afternoon (only in summer) and Sunday

You'll find this spot in a quiet *campiello* among the *callette* that thread their way around San Bartolomeo, but you'll have to go under a *sotopòrtego*. There are one or two tables outside. The *ombre* here are very good and served in the right glasses. But the *panini* are wonderful. Small, soft but slightly crunchy, they come with thirty or more different fillings. Choose from Tuscan cold cuts, chicken, lard and rosemary salad, alla carbonara with bacon, eggs and cheese, roast pork and *radicchio*, eggs and asparagus, goat's milk cheese and pistachios, courgettes and cheese or shrimp and *porcini* mushrooms. Your hosts live up to their name and can be decidedly... rustic.

Sahara [€ 26] 🖙 X ☀ ▶ B

041 721077, Cannaregio 2519, Fondamenta de la Misericordia ● 7 pm–12 pm (booking require at midday), closed Monday (winter only)

Situated on a lively, working-class *fondamenta*, the Sahara is the only ethnic eatery worth mentioning, particularly since it has moderate prices and serves meals until late. Rita and her husband Mouaffak in the kitchen will introduce you to their world of Arab and Syrian delights, such as falafel, small fried balls of chickpea flavoured with coriander and onion, magluba, rice with eggplant, minced beef, almonds and pine nuts served with yoghurt, and kebabs. The couscous can be ordered with meat, vegetables or fish. While away the longish wait – everything is cooked to order – by dipping pieces of khubz, flat white bread, in the delicious sauces made from chickpeas, eggplant, courgettes and yoghurt. A word of warning. There's belly dancing on Saturday.

San Barnaba ▮▮ ▶ F

041 5212754, Dorsoduro 2736, Calle Lunga San Barbara ● 11 am–3 pm and 6 pm–11 pm, closed Wednesday and Thursday morning

Despite its desolate air in the evening, Calle Lunga San Barnaba has plenty of attractive places where you can nibble something nice when the sun goes down. This is where you will find Sandro – for the time being at least, because he's always threatening to sell up and retire to Friuli – on duty behind an extensive counter laden with Veneto and Friulian delicacies. Try some of the *crostini* with *soprèssa*, smoked tuna ham or goose breast. But there's more. Luciana will also whip up hot food (€ 12-14), perhaps some stewed rabbit, *baccalà alla vicentina* or *figà a la venexiana*. The wines are tempting. Fans of Italian popular music might like to know that Sandro's father played bass with Fred Buscaglione.

CROSTINI CON SALAME, SPECK, PROSCIUTTO, FUNGHI, SALMONE, GAMBERETTI, ACCIUGHE

San Basilio [€ 42] ♥✕ ▶F

041 5210028, Dorsoduro 1516,
Fondamenta Zattere ☉ 9.30 am–10.30 pm,
closed Sunday and Monday

This is the ideal place to visit
after a stroll along one of Venice's favourite embankments. Right at the end of Fondamenta delle
Zattere, opposite the Mulino Stucky, Roberto and Stefano carry on the family business staying true
to the most traditional style of Venetian cuisine, particularly their spaghetti in cuttlefish ink and fried
whitebait. Booking ahead is highly recommended.

San Marco [€ 66] ✕♥♦★ ▶D

041 5285242, San Marco 1610, Frezzeria ☉ 12.30 pm–11 pm, closed Sunday

If you are on the verge of a panic attack in this ultra-touristy area, calm down again at San Marco, a
spacious *osteria con cucina* and *enoteca* that stays open until 11 at night. This means you can even have
a plate of spaghetti in the middle of the afternoon, if you feel the urge. The innovative menu combines
traditional flavours with seasonal ingredients. You might
find scallops with *prosecco* and courgettes, maltagliati pasta
with courgette flowers and shrimp, stuffed squid in mussel
sauce, monkfish in curry with green apple, pepper beef fillet
in coffee sauce or thin-sliced shin of venison with forest
fruits and star anise. Finish
off with a ginger *semifreddo*
dessert or a velvety chocolate
tenerina cake with *zabaione*.
The wine list is worth looking
at. This is also a good place
for a one-dish meal or a plate
of cheese and cold cuts at the
counter.

GUANCE DI VITELLO CON FUNGHI
E POLENTINA MORBIDA

Santa Marina [€ 59] ✕ ◗ ✳ ★ ▶ B, D

041 5285239, Castello 5911, Campo Santa Marina,
closed Sunday and Monday at midday

Two couples decided to join forces for
this venture into high-quality cuisine.
Agostino, Betty and Caterina busy
themselves in the kitchen while Danilo
serves at table. The quartet has earned
the admiration of many gourmets for
beautifully presented, extravagantly named dishes that are above all very, very good.
Tuna millefeuille with crispy artichokes, cuttlefish ink ravioli with *branzino* in a shellfish sauce,
fennel risotto with diced turbot and scampi in leek and ginger *saór* line up on the menu with
cream of borlotti beans with spicy tuna morsels. To finish your meal, there's the very popular
hot chocolate pie or the apple pie with cinnamon ice cream. For something more refreshing, try
the lemon sorbet with liquorice flakes. The wine list is attractive, as are the tables in the *campo*.

il Santo bevitore ⚲ ▼ ✳ ▶ B

041 717560, Cannaregio 2393a, Ponte Santa Fosca ● 7 am–11.30 pm, closed Saturday afternoon and evening

At last, a breeze of change is blowing through what was a rather run-down old *osteria* in a lovely
location just off the ever-busy Strada Nuova. Perch on one of the high stools with a generous *spritz* and
something to nibble with your aperitif, or at midday you might be tempted by a plate of pasta or a salad.
Beer and gin and tonics flow till late at night.

ai Storti ⚲ 🍷 ▶ B

041 2412255, San Polo 819, Calle San Mattio
🕒 9 am–3 pm and 6 pm–11 pm, closed Sunday

An *osteria con cucina* and a new stop on
the Rialto *giro di ombre*. The fried titbits on
the counter are scrumptious. Enjoy your
sardèle, *baccalà*, *mozzarelle in carrozza*,
meat or tuna *polpette* here or take some
home, if you feel so inclined. You can wash
your choice down with a good *ombréta*.
Alternatively, there are pasta or rice dishes
(€ 4-8) and classic *spienza*, *nervéti* and *baccalà in tècia*. When the aperitif hour comes round, ai Storti
fills up with over-sixties, who can recognise a good bar when they see one.

alle Testiere [€ 60] ✕ 🍴 ♥ ★ ▶ D

041 5227220, Castello 5801, Calle del Mondo Novo, closed Sunday and Monday

This tiny restaurant not far from Santa Maria Formosa continues its successful career, fusing the
interests of its two partners. Bruno in the kitchen is the aroma man. He lovingly prepares tiny *gnocchi*
with cinnamon-perfumed baby squid, *caparòssoli* sautéed with a hint of ginger, linguine with slivers
of monkfish, warm *gransèola*, and fillet of dory with aromatic herbs in orange and lemon sauce.
Everything is cooked with care, special attention being lavished on the selection of ingredients.
The same meticulousness is given to desserts. Don't miss the pear, ricotta and chocolate tart or
the *crema rosàda*. Luca is in charge of wine – his small selection speaks volumes for his thoughtful
approach – and he also supervises the cheese board. Some of the delights are escarun cuneese, verde
di Montegalda vicentina and buccia di rospo – the name means "toadskin" – a hard-to-come-by
Tuscan ewe's milk pecorino. What more could you ask? So remember to book well in advance.

_65

GUAZZETTO
DI MOLLUSCHI
E CROSTACEI

al Timon ⚲ ❢ ☀ ▶ A

340 2440245, Cannaregio 2754, Fondamenta degli Ormesini
● 11 am–3 pm and 6 pm–2 am, closed Monday

Alessandro has an architect brother and an enthusiastic father helping him now he has opened this welcoming *osteria* with good *ombre*, a range of *crostini* and one or two hot dishes. The habitués are often young music lovers, and the neighbours don't seem to mind. Our first impressions are promising so we'll be keeping an eye on it.

dai Tosi piccoli [€ 34] ✗ ❢ ☀ 🛵 ▶ H

041 5237102, Castello 738, Seco Marina
● 9.30 am–4 pm and 5 pm–11.30 pm, closed Wednesday

Just behind Via Garibaldi is this neighbourhood bar-cum-trattoria-cum-restaurant, which goes international during the Biennale festival. The young, go-getting management offers takeaway pizzas (€ 4-7), standard pastas for large, hungry tour groups, salads and meat or fish cooked on lava stone.

Tre scaini [€ 34] ✗ ❢ ☀ 🛵 ▶ G

041 5224790, Giudecca 53c, Calle Michelangelo,
closed Thursday and Monday evening

We're back in the heart of the Giudecca at a trattoria not far from the Zitelle. Most of the customers are working people or tourists who got on the wrong waterbus. You'll find substantial offerings for not very many euros – twelve, to be precise – before one o'clock. Fish and meat are on the menu in the evening. You must try the roast pork.

Tre spiedi – da Bes [€ 38] 🖙 ✗ ♥ ▶ B

041 5208035, Cannaregio 5906, Salizada San Cancian,
closed Sunday evening and Monday

This old-fashioned trattoria in a narrow *calletta* is run by two brothers. Genuine *rùsteghi*, they are married to two sisters and this friendly family team attracts a clientele of locals and particularly well-informed *forèsti*. Mixed fish starters, such as *latti di seppia* and *folpéti*, the traditional *saór*, spaghetti with *caparòssoli*, fish risottos and, of course, *baccalà*. To round things off, have a *sgropìn*. Bookings not accepted.

Vecio bragozzo [€ 46] 🔍✕☀ ▶B

041 5237277, Cannaregio 4386, Strada Nova, closed Monday

In its excellent, busy spot at the start of the Strada Nova, Vecio bragozzo is very popular with tourists. Some locals, too, are beginning to appreciate the value for money it offers. There are plenty of tables outside and the menu is traditional.

Vecio forner 👉✕❢ ▶F

041 5280424, Dorsoduro 671, Campo San Vio
● 8 am–9 pm, closed Sunday

A bar and osteria con *cucina*. The long counter has a wide range of salads, piadina flatbread sandwiches, toasted rolls, small pizzas and *polpette* as well as good, inexpensive pasta or rice dishes and traditional *secondi*, including tripe (€ 5-15). For dessert or as a mid-morning snack, have a soft, sweet ambrogino roll with hazelnut spread (€ 1.50). It is often busy at lunchtime but the young managers rise calmly above the chaos.

al Vecio fritoin [€ 50] ✕♥ ▶B

041 5222881, Santa Croce 2262, Calle della Regina, closed Monday

Despite the fact that it is featured in all the guidebooks, this is somewhere you can eat really well. Pasta and bread are made on the premises, ingredients are selected with meticulous care, service is friendly, portions generous and prices affordable. Irina and Wladi – from their names they could be a brace of Bulgarian gymnasts but both are as Venetian as they come – reel off the delights with enthusiasm. Mixed fish fry, grilled *canestrèi* or scallops, tuna or swordfish tartare, fried *moéche* with soft *polenta*, bavettine pasta in *saór*, fillet of sea bass with *porcini* mushrooms or lamb chops with vegetables. Wine list and cheese board are limited but very shrewdly selected.

INSALATA METELLO, DELLA NONNA E BRASILIANA;
MELANZANE IN SAÓR, FUNGHI ALLA RUSSA

Vini da Arturo [€ 82] ✕★ ▶ D

041 5286974, San Marco 3656, Calle dei Assassini,
closed Sunday (Saturday and Sunday in July)

So small some people call it the vagone, or "railway carriage", Vini da Arturo is nonetheless a quiet restaurant with a clientele of non-Venetians who come back regularly. For decades, Ernesto has been proudly declaiming his thankfully unchanging menu. Meat and vegetables are the main themes. Alessio prepares superb fillets of beef – with green pepper, strogonoff or voronoff – and the unique braciola a la venexiana, a chop for lovers of vinegar. The salads, served in small bowls, are irresistible, as are the eggplants in *saór*. Watch out for the spaghetti, beautifully cooked al dente, with chicory sauce or artichokes and to finish off the *tiramisù* cream or the chocolate mousse. A word of warning. Credit cards are not accepted.

Vini da Gigio [€ 52] ✕🥄♥★ ▶ B

041 5285140, Cannaregio 3628a, Fondamenta San Felice, closed Monday and Tuesday

Loved by many, sadly. This means you'll have to book well in advance. The small rooms with their equally small tables are the ideal place for couples or groups of friends looking for somewhere to eat well and chat in peace. No one will try to rush you and the service is exquisitely, serenely, unhurried. You can start from the truly impressive list of Italian and international wines and choose a menu to match, or let yourself be tempted by one of the many meat or fish dishes and accompany it with a wine proposed by the staff, whose suggestions are always spot-on. Specialties include the mixed fish *antipasto*, *baccalà* croquettes, beef *carpaccio*, penne pasta with *gransèola* or gorgonzola and pistachios, grilled eel, fried fish, masorino alla buranella (Burano-style duck) or *figà a la venexiana*. Make sure you try the puddings or a fruit crostata (tart). There's also an interesting selection of craft beers, whiskies and grappas from Veneto and Friuli.

Vino vino [€ 32/60] X♟️🍷 ▶ D

041 2417688, San Marco 2007a, Calle della Veste ⏺ 10.30 am–11.30 pm, closed Tuesday

Vino vino was originally intended to be a wine bar attached to the Antico Martini restaurant, whose kitchens and cellars it uses. In fact, it has done so well that it is now better known than its parent. You will find a wide range of excellent wines by the glass and the counter offers an equally satisfying range of food. Select from octopus salad, oven-baked pasta, *pasta e fasiòi*, *baccalà* either *alla vicentina* or creamed, quail with *polenta*, roast rabbit or guinea fowl, veal stew, meatballs with mushrooms, chine of suckling pig, beef stewed in Barolo or sautéed veal kidneys.

It's a great place for a quick bite without wasting time among busy diners and tightly packed tables. Service can sometimes be a tad offhand but it's worth the sacrifice.

Vinus 🍷🍶 ▶ C

041 715004, Dorsoduro 3961, Calle del Scaleter ⏺ 10.30 am–3 pm and 5 pm–1 am, closed Sunday morning

A lovely modern *enoteca* located between the Frari and the Santa Margherita area.

There are plenty of wines and classic *crostini* to nibble at the counter as you listen to generally

good music. Popular when the weather is not so good. Thursday night is jazz night and there are oysters on Friday.

Vivaldi [€ 47] 🔍✕🍷 ▶D

041 5238185, San Polo 1457, Calle de la Madoneta
● 11.30 am–2.30 pm and 6.30 pm–10.30 pm, closed Wednesday

In one of those very narrow *calli* where Venetians ruin their coats on the walls as they avoid the main tourist routes, you can find a nice hot plate of food to sit down to – tagliolini with lemon sauce, spaghetti with cuttlefish ink, Venetian-style liver or thin-sliced beef with rosemary – or you can stand at the counter for some baby cuttlefish or octopus, a *polpetta* or a *crostino* with *baccalà*. The setting is very traditional, with dressers, wooden tables and all the trimmings.

Vitae 🖙✕🍷☀ ▶D

041 5205205, San Marco 4118, Salizada San Luca
● 9 am–1.30 am, closed Saturday morning and Sunday

A modern ambience and some tables outside in the *calletta*, Vitae is a magnet at midday for young professionals and office workers around Campo San Luca who enjoy the one-dish meals on offer

70–

(€ 6-8). There's pork with boiled rice, chicken morsels with *castraùre* and octopus salad with celery, cherry tomatoes and courgettes. If you prefer, try the tempting *crostini* and little *tramezzini* with roast pork, chicory, smoked speck ham, mushrooms, olives, tuna or vegetarian fillings. Now that the thirty-somethings have moved to the far side of the bridge in the evening, this has become the meeting place for techno-alternative twenty-year-olds as they sip mojitos, caipirinhas, margaritas, cuba libres or daiquiris and nibble olives or dip into dips.

Wine bar 🍷✕🍴 ▶C

Santa Croce 466/d, Fondamenta Sant'Andrea ● 7 am–10 pm, closed Sunday

A good place to meet near Piazzale Roma is always useful, the more so if it is a bar and *enoteca* where you can take the edge off your appetite with a mini *panino* and a glass of good wine courteously served. In the middle of the day, there is hot food for those with more time and a bigger space to fill.
You can try the cannelloni, the *pasticcio,* tripe in parmesan cheese or *muséto.*

da Zorzi [€ 16/70] 🔍✗❦ ▶D

041 5204589, Calle dei Fuseri, San Marco 4359, closed Sunday

This is a nice place but it seems to be in two minds
about pricing. It's perfect at lunchtime if you're
on a budget. For € 16, you can tuck into penne
alla carbonara or with tomato and chicory, and
then steamed cuttlefish or a grilled steak. In the
evening, things get pricier, although the traditional

fare on offer – pasta with artichokes, potato stew – is carefully prepared.
If you like, you can just prop up the bar and enjoy an *ombréta*.

alla Zucca [€ 39] 🖝✗🍴☀♥ ▶C

041 5241570, Santa Croce 1762, Ponte del Megio, closed Sunday

A classic. The warm, quiet interior has wood-panelled walls,
benches to sit on and a few tables outside at the foot of the bridge.
Imagination – tempered with moderation – rules. Service is
pleasingly informal and the cuisine is inventive but not slapdash.
There are lots of vegetables, some with hint of the orient:

couscous with spicy meat balls, roast lamb
chops in tzatziki sauce, a vegetarian dish with
rice and sesame, pumpkin flan with mature
ricotta, pork in ginger with pilaf rice and, to
finish your meal, fig ice cream with caramel
or mint and chocolate *semifreddo*.
The wine list covers all of Italy and speaks
volumes for the effort that went into
compiling it. Book in advance.

... near Venice

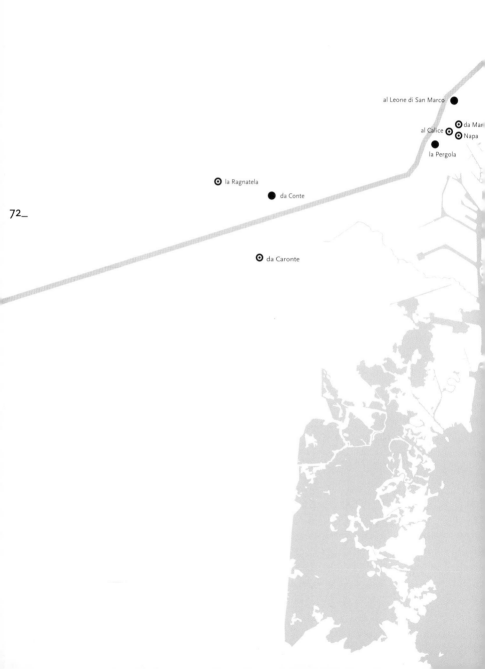

al Leone di San Marco ●

al Calice ⊙ ⊙ da Mar
⊙ Napa

● la Pergola

⊙ la Ragnatela

● da Conte

⊙ da Caronte

la Ostaria

locanda Cipriani

alla Maddalena

da Romano
al Gatto nero

Tedeschi

Busa la Torre

−73

alle Vignole

Beerbante

Afrika

bar Trento

da Nane

da Memo

Celeste

islands

Murano

Dizzy after visiting dozens of shops full of glittering glassware and stunned by the splendour of the church of Santi Maria e Donato – a must-see – you'll be needing something to eat. You could be in for a pleasant surprise.

Busa la Torre [€ 48] ✕ ☀

041 739662, Campo Santo Stefano 3, open all week at midday only (occasionally on Friday evening)

Lele is the gentle giant who greets you in this airy, open *campo* where you can be sure of a pleasant meal break. The seasonal, fish-based menu boasts tagliatelle with *canòce* or shrimp and *porcini* mushrooms, sea bass ravioli with *gransèola* sauce and, of course, Lele's legendary fried *moeche*.

Sant'Erasmo and Vignole

These two islands have always been Venice's market garden, supplying the city with fresh vegetables, including some very special products such as *castraùre*. Today, both are also places where Venetians like to come to spend some time in the open air in a green setting.

Tedeschi [€ 30] ✕ ☀

041 5203346, Sant'Erasmo, Torre di Massimiliano ● 10 am–11 pm, open all week

Alessandro was born and bred in this corner of the lagoon. Now he is taking over an establishment that offers an anthropologically interesting mix of humanity. You might see some of the taciturn workmen who have been repairing the island's sea defences for the past few years, families who are spending the day at the *bacàn* or tourists advised to come to look at the fortifications by slightly sadistic friends. The menu includes pizzas and various fish dishes. Everything is self service.

alle Vignole (vecchie) [€ 37] ✕ ❢ ☀ 🛥

041 5289707, Isola delle Vignole 12a ● 10 am–11 pm, closed Monday (open April to September)

This is a favourite with small boat owners and pleasure rowers. It's not easy to reach by public transport. From the waterbus landing, carry straight on, then turn right across the bridge and follow the signs across the fields.

You'll find the delicious fish or meat grills served with seasonal vegetables from the nearby fields. Pizzas from a wood-fired oven (€ 5-8) supplement the wide range of food on the counter, which includes turbot, eel, monkfish, *mazzancolle*, cuttlefish, bass, sea bream and sole, as well as beef or horse ribs, spare ribs, chicken and grilled sausages. You sit down to eat at long tables outside and food is available all day.

Burano

Beautiful, colourful Burano offers a unique atmosphere and also two outstanding traditional trattorias with paintings on the walls, high ceilings and white tablecloths. The patrons are families with grandparents in tow and substantial numbers of tourists who have, truth to tell, tarnished the spirit of place.

Cast your votes for ...

da Romano [€ 60] ✗ ☀

041 730030, Piazza Galuppi 221, closed Sunday evening and Tuesday

The better known of the two establishments, located in the former lace school. The menu features the freshest of fish, shellfish and crustaceans from the lagoon, mixed fries and mixed grills. This is the place to come if traditional is what you're looking for.

al Gatto nero [€ 66] ✗ ☀

041 730120, Fondamenta Giudecca 88, closed Monday

Ruggero's kitchen also serves super-fresh fish, selected by the man himself. The ambience is friendly and very Burano. You can eat the best *risotto di gò* in the Venetian archipelago but don't forget the *antipasti*, the fried fish or some craft-made biscuits to round off your meal. Afterwards, go out the back door and lie on the grass to enjoy the view.

Mazzorbo

You can walk over the Ponte Longo bridge from Burano to sleepy Mazzorbo, a green island of gardens and villas with characteristic chimneys. It's a lovely place to stroll or relax under the trees if you've been walking around all day.

alla Maddalena [€ 36] ☛ ✗ ☀

041 730151, Mazzorbo 7b, closed Thursday (booking required in the evening)

Opposite the Mazzorbo waterbus stop is this traditional fish restaurant, where in summer you can sit beside the canal, laze under the bowers or relax in the quiet garden behind the restaurant. When the hunting season begins in September, the menu includes feathered game, most of which is shot in the lagoon's *vàlli* (you'll have to book in advance), and often other winter favourites such as tripe soup and *pasta e fasiòi*.

Torcello

A magical spot where the lagoon's unique beauty is enhanced by its most ancient architectural and artistic treasures. A trip to Torcello is a must, preferably during the week.

locanda Cipriani [€ 89] ✗ ▼ ♦ ☀ ⚔ ♥ ★

041 730150, Piazza Santa Fosca 29, ● 11 am–10 pm, closed Monday evening and Tuesday

Justly famous and ever elegant, locanda Cipriani discreetly avoids any ostentation, which would be quite out of place on Torcello. Management is in the hands of the impeccable Bonifacio. Looking onto a meticulously cared-for garden and the church of Santa Fosca, you can savour the kitchen's classics, such as risotto alla torcellana (with estuary grown vegetables), spiced scampi tails with pilaf rice, fillet of sole with artichokes and a meringue that is close to perfection. If you come here in the middle of the afternoon, preferably after a boat trip round the island, sit down to a luxurious cup of hot chocolate with a peerless millefeuille. If you can afford it, stay overnight in one of the rooms, which magically combine simplicity with irresistibly seductive appeal.

Lido

This is where Venetians go to the seaside in summer. If they have a beach hut, they head for the central beaches. Those who haven't go to either end of the island. We'll only include three addresses that stand apart from the mass of resort-style restaurants.
All three are informal, unpretentious and vaguely alternative.

Beerbante [€ 40] ⚲ ✕ ☀ ⚯

041 5262550, Piazzale Ravà 12, closed Monday (closed in the evening Monday to Thursday in winter)

There's nothing better than a nice big plate of grilled meat or fish, a salad and cool beer after you've been touching up your tan all day on the nearby beach. Large groups welcome.

Afrika [€ 36] ✕ ☀

041 5260186, Via Lazzaro Mocenigo 9, closed Tuesday

A trattoria frequented by regulars and the occasional lost tourist. Meat and fish are on the menu. There's a good mixed fish *antipasto*, a few pasta and rice options, then you could have fried scampi and squid with a glass of cool Collio wine.

Bar Trento [€ 32] ☞ ✕ ☀

041 5265960, Via Sandro Gallo 82e ☉ 7 am–9 pm (until 11 pm in summer), closed Sunday

A genuine working-class *osteria* with a counter that is laden – round the clock – with *baccalà*, *folpéti*, *bovoléti*, *cotechino* sausage and *nervéti* with onion. The kitchen is open only at midday for the ravenous workers who sit down at the tables under the bowers for a substantial lunch.
Evening meals are served during the cinema festival, when the Bar Trento is also open on Sundays.

Pellestrina

The island of Pellestrina is a narrow, and at times very narrow, strip of land that separates the southern lagoon from the open sea. Its charming atmosphere is the setting for some fine fresh fish restaurants, just the thing after a boat trip or a cycle run from Lido.
We'll mention three large, classic restaurants that locals often take over for christenings or confirmations. Everyone has a favourite.

da Celeste [€ 42] ✕ ☀

041 967355, Sestiere Vianelli 625b, closed Wednesday (open March to October)

This must be the loveliest terrace in the south lagoon.
The fish is fresh and the village of Pellestrina is delightful.

da Nane [€ 48] ✕ ☀

041 5279100, San Pietro in Volta 282, closed Monday (open April to November)

Another terrace overlooking the lagoon and more super-fresh fish.
Other specialties include *gnocchetti* with scampi and the superb fish *pasticcio*.

da Memo [€ 48] ✕ ☀

041 5279125, San Pietro in Volta 157 ☉ 8 am–12 pm closed Tuesday (open March to December)

This restaurant with outside tables in an attractive garden stands on the Portosecco bend.
At the counter you'll find *polpettine*, canapés and other *cichèti*.

Mainland

Venetians go to the mainland for pleasure, perhaps for a boat trip along the Brenta, or because they have to. When you live in the middle of a lagoon, it's not always easy to find the right washer for your leaking bathroom tap.

But whatever your motive, it's useful to have the addresses of one or two good places to eat.

Marcon

la Osteria [€ 30 carne/54 pesce] ✕ ▮ ✳ ★

041 5950068, Piazza 4 Novembre 9, closed Monday (Saturday and Sunday, open evenings only)

This fine eatery has been open in the main square at Marcon for the past couple of years. The atmosphere is homely and there are a few tables outside. Inside or out, you will enjoy Renato's creations, such as pumpkin cream with chanterelle mushrooms and a parmesan cheese wafer, octopus and celery terrine, eggplant pie with mozzarella and tomato or fresh pasta with red mullet and wild fennel. The fish and meat *secondi* are unambitious but well prepared and the desserts, often puddings, are all made on the premises. Those seeking something special on the wine list or cheese board will be pleasantly surprised. Giovanna has more than two hundred and fifty wines and the care that has gone into selecting the cheeses is obvious. If you appreciate top quality, this is where to come to find it.

–77

Mestre

al Calice [€ 32] ✕ ▼ ▮ ✳ ★

041 986100, Piazza Ferretto 70b, ● 9 am–3 pm and 5 pm–1 am (until 9 pm on Sunday), open all week

In their welcoming courtyard with attractive wooden tables, Emiliano, Maurizio and Marco run a much admired *enoteca-osteria*. As you pass through Piazza Ferretto, it's hard to resist popping in for a *cichèto* at the well-stocked counter. Wash it down with a glass of one of the many wines on offer. There's a tempting menu if you prefer a sit-down meal. The *antipasto* might be boiled fish, marinaded fish or selected cold cuts. The *primi* and *secondi* are classics, like tagliolini with *porcini* mushrooms, *baccalà alla vicentina*, grilled sea bass or thin sliced beef, and the salads are skilfully prepared. The wine list features six hundred bottles.

da Mariano [€ 32] ☞ ✕ ▼ ▮ ♥ ★

041 615427 – 615765, Via Spalti 49 corner of Via Cecchini 1, open midday and evenings from Wednesday to Friday, closed Sunday

Antonio, his wife Nadia and their son have managed to transform father Mariano's old *osteria* into one of Mestre's most exciting eateries. Not far from Piazza Ferretto, da Mariano offers a welcoming atmosphere and excellent value for money, as well as a two hundred-label wine list and good house wines, a fine selection of cheeses, cold meats and spirits, pasta made on the premises and a territory-dedicated cuisine. Offerings include biancoperla maize *polenta* with morlacco cheese, pasta with chicory and pumpkin, braised beef jowl, Marano flour and chanterelle mushroom tart, pasta alla carlina (with capers, tomatoes and gherkins) and *baccalà* alla cappuccina (with pine nuts and sultanas). Antonio organises regular themed tastings.

al Leone di San Marco [€ 52] ×

041 5341742, Via Trezzo 6, Carpenedo, closed Sunday evening and Monday

If you like old-fashioned, tasty, no-frills cooking, head for the centre of Carpenedo, where there's a great place that other guides have already featured. The fish is locally caught and wonderfully fresh.

Napa ×☀️▮

041 5042206, Via Lazzari 2, ● 7.30 am–12 pm, closed Sunday

Sophisticated erudition is the theme from breakfast time to last orders. The book-length wine list embraces sparklers, champagnes, some of them biodynamic (which doesn't mean they are made using alternative energy sources), beers, mineral waters, rums and other spirits. There are nice things to nibble at the tables outside, including club sandwiches, pancakes with taleggio cheese, pork fillet marinaded with fennel and parmesan. It's a tad snobbish but very fashionable and right in the centre.

la Pergola [€ 37] ☞×▮

041 974932, Via Fiume 42, closed Saturday morning and Sunday (closed Saturday evening in summer)

If it wasn't for the line of SUVs and jeeps parked at the entrance – nobody would dream of actually walking those extra few metres – it wouldn't be easy to find this anonymous little building in the heart of the garden city. There are twenty or so tables and a long counter. Davide, the cheese fanatic, is in charge in the kitchen while Paolo looks after the tables and the wine. Fresh pasta and traditional-style meat and vegetable dishes are often joined by innovative offerings. There might be tagliolini with rabbit and thyme sauce, pappardelle pasta with broad beans and pecorino cheese, loin of lamb with chanterelle mushrooms, morsels of veal with citrus fruit and ginger, braised veal jowl, cannellini beans in saffron sauce and *fiorentina* steaks.

The cheese trolley, with raw goat's milk and blue cheeses, and the wine list are equal to the situation, as is the brief but mouth-watering menu of sweets made on the premises, such as fig and Montagnana ham tart, chocolate mousse or Neapolitan pastiera cake.

Preganziol

Ombre rosse [€ 34] ☞×☀️▮

0422 490037, Via Franchetti 78, San Trovaso ● 6 pm–2 am, closed Sunday

This restaurant is worth the detour. At least, that's what the many Venetians who come here think, even though Tessa and Claudio's establishment is almost at Treviso. What diners find here is a tradition-inspired kitchen that blends experience with a touch of imagination. The menu is short but varied, with fish, meat and vegetable dishes. There's Badoere asparagus, bean soup with *radicchio di Treviso*, mushrooms and truffles, swordfish with capers and pine nuts or baked tuna, but look out for couscous and bahmi goreng. The cold meats are mouth-watering, the cheese trolley is splendid and there are a thousand wines waiting to be uncorked.

It's easy to see why discriminating Venetians venture this far.

Riviera del Brenta

la Ragnatela [€ 24/42] ☞×♦ ☀♥
041 436050, Via Caltana 79, Scaltenigo – Mirano, closed on Wednesday

No, you didn't take a wrong turning. This unprepossessing building is the home of workers' co-operative where Galdino and his team serve top quality cuisine that is sure to delight. The menu ranges from the solidly traditional (*baccalà*, *saór* and *moéche*) to highly professional experimental dishes closely tied to the seasons and the products of the territory. You might find shrimp savor, a fourteenth-century Venetian delicacy, lasagna with crustacean sauce, ginger juice and chanterelle mushroom velouté, breast of mallard duck with orange and coffee sauce on a salad of pears, pumpkin-filled tortelli creamed with foie gras, thin-sliced duck with morello cherries, pigeon stuffed with plums and so on through to the cinnamon mousse with pears in red wine or spiced ice cream with a sesame wafer and hazelnut and caramel sauce. The wine list is shrewdly constructed, featuring three hundred Italian and international labels. We recommend the "spider's web" wholeheartedly.

da Caronte [€ 32] ☞×♦ ☀
041 412091, Via Dolo 39, Paluello di Stra, closed Tuesday evening and Wednesday

A restaurant, much patronised by locals, with pleasant tables outside. The menu puts seasonal vegetables firmly in the foreground. Note that the delicious fruit tarts, bread and pasta are all made on the premises. Highlights include pumpkin *gnocchi*, ravioli with *carletti* and *bruscàndoli*, tagliata (thin sliced) ostrich and morsels of pony with *radicchio di Treviso*. There are about fifty wines on the list and over a hundred and thirty grappas.

da Conte [€ 30/50] ×♦ ☀♥
041 479571, Via Caltana 133, Marano, closed Sunday and Monday

Turn left after the underpass and there you are. This tastefully restored country house is where Manuela and Giorgio prepare their varied seasonal cuisine, highlighting the freshness and natural aromas of the ingredients. Some dishes are traditional while others come from the pair's private cookbook.
Look for *bìgoli* with duck sauce, pork jowl in red wine, leg of goose braised with baby onions and pumpkin, pan-fried pumpkin and shrimp in cinnamon, tartare of *oràda*, pappardelle pasta in aromatic herbs, pine nuts and pecorino cheese, saddle of rabbit in cardamom with melon salad and, to round off your meal, ginger ice cream with mango and coconut sauce or *zabaione* with dried-grape moscato passito wine. The wine list has three hundred entries and there is a selection of cheeses.
During the week, the midday menu is more competitively priced.

eateries by price category

– forèsti establishments in italics –

inexpensive	affordable
Frary's bar [€ 22]	la Pergola [€ 37]
los Murales [€ 15/30]	alle Vignole (vecchie) [€ 37]
alle Due gondolette [€ 24]	alla Botte [€ 37]
Pontini – da Giada e Roberta [€ 25]	Ruga Rialto [€ 37]
Sahara [€ 26]	al Diporto [€ 38]
Cea [€ 28]	al Nono risorto [€ 38]
ai Osti [€ 30]	ai Quaranta ladroni [€ 38]
Tedeschi [€ 30]	Quatro feri [€ 38]
dalla Marisa [€ 27 €/36]	Tre spiedi – da Bes [€ 38]
da Alberto [€ 32]	Ca' d'Oro – alla Vedova [€ 39]
Ganesh Ji [€ 32]	alla Zucca [€ 39]
al Faro [€ 32]	Beerbante [€ 39]
al Garanghélo (1) [€ 32]	la Bitta [€ 40]
Bar Trento [€ 32]	Pane, vino e San Daniele [€ 40]
al Calice [€ 32]	da Conte [€ 30/50]
da Mariano [€ 32]	Algiubagiò [€ 25/56]
da Caronte [€ 32]	ae Cravate [€ 42]
Canottieri [€ 20/44]	la Osteria [€ 30/54]
Cavatappi [€ 18/42]	da Celeste [€ 42]
a la Campana [€ 17/48]	San Basilio [€ 42]
la Ragnatela [€ 24/42]	Oniga [€ 43]
Bandierette [€ 34]	da Zorzi [€ 16/70]
alla Frasca [€ 18/50]	Muro [€ 35/52]
Gislon [€ 34]	Anice stellato [€ 44]
Ombre rosse [€ 34]	da Bepi – già 54 [€ 44]
alla Palanca [€ 34]	alla Madonna [€ 44]
al Portego [€ 34]	Rioba [€ 45]
dai Tosi piccoli [€ 34]	Vecio bragozzo [€ 46]
Tre scaini [€ 34]	ae Do spade [€ 46]
Fontana [€ 35]	Vino vino [€ 32/60]
da Mario [€ 35]	al Bacco [€ 47]
Afrika [€ 35]	Cantinone storico [€ 47]
Birraria [€ 36]	al Fontego dei pescaori [€ 47]
da Pinto [€ 36]	da Ignazio [€ 47]
alla Maddalena [€ 36]	Vivaldi [€ 47]

80_

budget-threatening	exclusive
al Garanghélo (2) [€ 48]	Acquapazza [€ 78]
Mistrà [€ 48]	Centrale [€ 80]
il Refolo [€ 48]	Vini da Arturo [€ 82]
Busa la torre [€ 48]	al Covo [€ 84]
da Memo [€ 48]	Monaco – Gran canal [€ 85]
l'Angolo di Tanit [€ 49]	ai Gondolieri [€ 86]
Altanella [€ 50]	locanda Cipriani [€ 89]
al Diavolo e l'acqua santa [€ 50]	da Fiore [€ 120]
alla Mascareta [€ 50]	Harry's bar [€ 210]
al Vecio fritoin [€ 50]	
Corte sconta [€ 52]	
Vini da Gigio [€ 52]	
al Leone di San Marco [€ 52]	
all'Aciugheta [€ 54]	
Bea vita [€ 54]	
da Alvise [€ 55]	
al Mascaron [€ 55]	
Boccadoro [€ 58]	
da Nane [€ 58]	
Santa Marina [€ 59]	
Antiche carampane [€ 60]	
Antico giardinetto [€ 60]	
Linea d'ombra [€ 60]	
Mirai [€ 60]	
da Romano [€ 60]	
alle Testiere [€ 60]	
agli Alboretti [€ 63]	
Avogaria [€ 63]	
al Bacaro [€ 64]	
San Marco [€ 66]	
al Gatto Nero [€ 66]	
Fiaschetteria toscana [€ 70]	

a glossary of venexiàn (and Italian)

words ancient, old and new — an informal collection

aciughéta (plural **aciughéte**) anchovy

al cartoccio (standard Italian) baked in a sealed parcel of paper or foil

àmolo (plural **àmoli**) damson

ànara (plural **ànare**) duck (October-November)

anguèla (plural **anguèle**) sand smelt (*Atherina boyeri*), a small fish commonly found in the lagoon, also called *acquadella*

antipasto (plural **antipasti**: standard Italian) a starter

arancìno (plural **arancìni**: standard Italian) ball of rice mixed with chopped meat, ham or cheese, breaded and fried

armelìn (plural **armelìni**) apricot

articiòco (plural **articiòchi**) artichoke

asià spiny dogfish (*Mustelus vulgaris*)

àstese (plural **àstesi**) common lobster (*Homarus gammarus*)

bacàn lagoon beach on the island of Sant'Erasmo, near the harbour mouth of Lido, with shallow seabed and large areas that emerge at low tide; much loved by Venetians, who bring their children – and plenty of baked pasta – here at the first sign of sunshine

bàcaro (plural **bàcari**) see **osteria**

baccalà (standard Italian) dried cod

baccalà alla vicentina dried cod cooked Vicenza style in tomatoes and olives

baccalà mantecato boiled stockfish, flaked, steamed, aromatised with garlic and parsley, and then blended with oil, like a mayonnaise, until creamy

bagìgi peanuts

BRUSCÀNDOLI

baìcoli dry Venetian biscuits, rusk-like in appearance

baìcolo young sea bass (*Dicentrarchus labrax*)

barbòn red mullet (*Mullus surmuletus*) (September-November)

barbunsàl calf's chin, boiled with carrots and celery, then dressed cold with oil and vinegar

barèna (plural **barène**) sandbank or land normally submerged at high tide with vegetation emerging above the water level

baùta (plural **baùte**) Carnival mask comprising a black hood and lace cape

bechèr (plural **bechèri**) butcher

bevaràssa (plural **beveràsse**) cockle (*Chamelea gallina*) or clam (US) (all year)

bievaròl grocer's

bìgoli large coarse spaghetti, usually made with wholemeal wheat, used for **bìgoli in salsa** – the **salsa** is made by gently frying onions and anchovies with a little white wine or vinegar; once, this was a traditional meal on days of abstinence from meat

birìn smallest measure of beer (about 10 cc)

birèta small glass of beer (about 20 cc)

bisàto (plural **bisàti**) adult eel (*Anguilla anguilla*) (August-November)

bìsi peas

bòcolo (plural **bòcoli**) rosebud, traditionally given by young men to their lady loves on 25 April

bògio boiling

CARLETTI

bòsega grey mullet (*Chelon labrosus*) (September-October)

bovoléto (plural **bovoléti**) snails served with garlic and parsley as **cichèti**

bòvolo (plural **bòvoli**) spiral; the name has been transferred to the snail and the traditional round Venetian bread roll

branzino sea bass (*Dicentrarchus labrax*), a much prized species of fish (July-December)

brìcola (plural **brìcole**) wooden pole set in the lagoon to mark off a canal, or for use as a mooring

bruscàndoli wild hop buds used in risottos and other dishes (April)

bruschetta (plural **bruschette**: standard Italian) slice of bread toasted and rubbed with garlic, then drizzled with olive oil

bucatini (standard Italian) hollow, spaghetti-like pasta

burrata (standard Italian) a stretched cheese envelope filled with cream of whey

bùsara scampi sauce, originally from Dalmatia

bussolài buranèi (Burano) ring-shaped biscuits made with egg (the S-shaped variations are known as **esse buranèi**), for dunking into wine

bussolài ciosòti the Chioggia version of the biscuit is not sweet

butiro butter

calle (plural **calli**; diminutive **calletta**) a narrow Venetian street

campo (plural **campi**; diminutive **campiello**) a Venetian square

canarìn a traditional yellowish digestive drink made by soaking lemon rind in hot water

canestrèlo (plural **canestrèi** or **canestrèli**) small scallop (*Aequipecten opercularis*) (September-October)

FIORI DI ZUCCA

cannolo (plural **cannoli**: standard Italian) tube-shaped, cream-filled Sicilian sweets

canòce mantis prawn (*Squilla mantis*) (September-November)**capalònga** or **càpa da dèo** razor shell (*Ensis minor*) (September-October)

caparòssoli cross-cut carpet shell (*Tapes decussatus*), known as *vongola verace* in standard Italian (all year)

capasanta fan shell scallop (*Pecten jacobaeus*) or St James' shell, or coquilles Saint-Jacques in French (October-November); Venetian scallops are smaller and tastier

càpatonda or **margaròta** a bivalve mollusc (*Cerastoderma glaucum*) found on the lagoon bed and sandbars

caragòl generic name for various species (*Gibbula* spp) of winkle-like molluscs with pointed, helical shells; changing environmental conditions have caused a dramatic fall in their numbers

carbòna a pied-à-terre, or rather a garçonnière

carèga (plural **carèghe**) chair

carletti spring herbs used to flavour risottos and omelettes

carpaccio (standard Italian) thin slices of raw meat or fish

_83

CASTRAÙRE

BÌSI

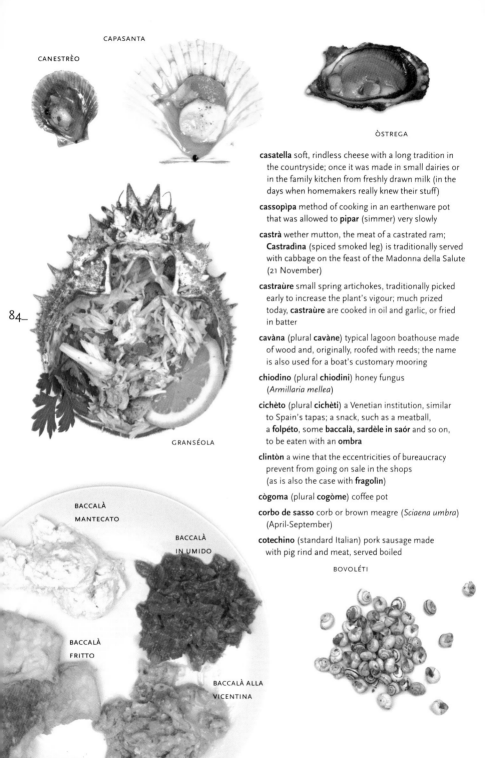

CANESTRÈO

CAPASANTA

ÒSTREGA

GRANSÉOLA

casatella soft, rindless cheese with a long tradition in the countryside; once it was made in small dairies or in the family kitchen from freshly drawn milk (in the days when homemakers really knew their stuff)

cassopìpa method of cooking in an earthenware pot that was allowed to pipar (simmer) very slowly

castrà wether mutton, the meat of a castrated ram; Castradìna (spiced smoked leg) is traditionally served with cabbage on the feast of the Madonna della Salute (21 November)

castraùre small spring artichokes, traditionally picked early to increase the plant's vigour; much prized today, castraùre are cooked in oil and garlic, or fried in batter

cavàna (plural cavàne) typical lagoon boathouse made of wood and, originally, roofed with reeds; the name is also used for a boat's customary mooring

chiodino (plural chiodini) honey fungus (Armillaria mellea)

cichèto (plural cichèti) a Venetian institution, similar to Spain's tapas; a snack, such as a meatball, a folpéto, some baccalà, sardèle in saór and so on, to be eaten with an ombra

clintòn a wine that the eccentricities of bureaucracy prevent from going on sale in the shops (as is also the case with fragolìn)

cògoma (plural cogòme) coffee pot

corbo de sasso corb or brown meagre (Sciaena umbra) (April-September)

cotechino (standard Italian) pork sausage made with pig rind and meat, served boiled

BACCALÀ
MANTECATO

BACCALÀ
IN UMIDO

BACCALÀ
FRITTO

BACCALÀ ALLA
VICENTINA

BOVOLÉTI

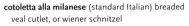

CAPELÓNGHE

BEVARÀSSE   CAPARÒSSOLI

cotoletta alla milanese (standard Italian) breaded veal cutlet, or wiener schnitzel

cràf the Venetian version of doughnuts, called *krapfen* in Italian

crèma frìta a custard of eggs, milk, flour and sugar, covered in breadcrumbs and then fried

crema rosada a custard of milk, eggs, sugar and vanilla

cren horseradish sauce, served with boiled meats

crostata (plural crostate: standard Italian) uncovered tart of shortcrust pastry, usually topped with jam, fruit or custard

crostino (plural crostini: standard Italian) small piece of toasted bread with a savoury topping

curasàn the idiosyncratic Venetian pronunciation of croissant

dìndio turkey

durèlo (plural durèli) chicken gizzard

enoteca (plural enoteche: standard Italian) wine shop, often selling food and wine by the glass

fasiòl (plural fasiòi) kidney bean

fèlze the small cabin that was once mounted on gondolas

fenòcio (plural fenòci) fennel

figà liver; Venetian style liver, or figà a la venexiàna (standard Italian *fegato alla veneziana*), is thinly sliced calf's liver cooked with onions over a low flame

finferlo (plural finferli) chanterelle mushroom (*Cantharellus cibarius*)

fiorentina (plural fiorentine: standard Italian) T-bone steak

fiori di zucca (standard Italian) courgette flowers

foghèr hearth

fòlaga (plural fòlaghe) coot; when the birds ate only fish, their meat acquired an unpleasant flavour; now that they are farmed and given feed, they have become a delicacy

forèsto (plural forèsti) a non-Venetian; the term is applied to anyone who lives *al di là del ponte...* (beyond the bridge) on the mainland

fòrfe scissors

folpéto (plural folpéti) baby or *moscardino* octopus (*Eledone moschata*) with a single row of suckers on the tentacles (October-November); folpéti cònsi are baby octopus boiled in water with carrots and celery, then cut in half lengthways and seasoned with oil, lemon juice, salt and pepper

fólpo (plural fólpi) common octopus (*Octopus vulgaris*), with two rows of suckers on the tentacles

_85

CALAMÀRO

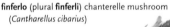

SCAMPI

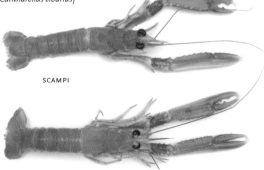

ALICI MARINATE

SARDÈLE IN SAÓR

fondamenta (plural **fondamente**) paved street running alongside a canal or the lagoon

fondo di carciofo (plural **fondi di carciofo**: standard Italian) what is left over from an artichoke after you have removed all the leaves and the stem; **fondi di carciofo** can be purchased at the market already trimmed and ready to be cooked in a **tècia** with garlic and parsley

fragolìn wine made from fragola grapes; its sale is illegal

frègola (plural **frègole**) crumb

fritoìn fried fish stall; sadly, there are none left

frìtola (plural **frìtole**) fritter with raisins and pine nuts, traditionally made for Carnival

fugàssa (plural **fugàsse**: standard Italian *focaccia*, plural *focacce*) flat bread

fulminante (plural **fulminanti**) match

galàni sweet dough rolled very thin and fried, traditionally made for Carnival

ganasséta (plural **ganasséte**) cheek

garanghélo convivial meal with friends

garùsolo (plural **garùsoli**) sea snail (*Bolinus brandaris*) served as an appetiser; the animal is extracted from the shell with a toothpick and eaten fresh (June-September)

giro di òmbre pre-prandial stroll round the local **osterie**, sampling an **òmbra** and a **cichèto** in each

gnocchetti (standard Italian) small **gnocchi**

gnocchi (standard Italian) potato dumplings

gò goby (*Zosterisessor ophiocephalus*) (October-March)

golosèsso (plural **goloséssi**) a titbit or delicacy

gòto (plural **gòti**) glass

gransèola (plural **gransèole**) spiny spider crab (*Maja squinado*); the carapace can be as large as 20 cm across (October-December); after it has been boiled, cleaned and dressed with oil, garlic, parsley and lemon, the flesh is then reinserted into the shell and served

grànso (plural **grànsi**) common shore crab (*Carcinus mediterraneus*), frequent in the lagoon; it is called *masanéta*, *spiàntano* or *moéca*, depending on its stage of development

gròpo (plural **gròpi**) knot

latti di seppia (literally "cuttlefish milk") cuttlefish (*Sepia officinalis*) eggs

lièvaro (plural **lièvari**) hare

linguine (standard Italian) long, flat pasta

lugànega (plural **lugàneghe**) long fresh pork sausage, served with rice (*rìsi*)

SÈPE IN NERO
CON POLENTA

SCHÌE CON
POLENTINA MORBIDA

INSALATA DI FÒLPI

SEPPIOLINE SOGLIOLA TRIGLIE SARDÈLE MOÉCHE

maneghèto (plural maneghèti) beer served in glass
with handle (about 20 cc)

maràntega (plural marànteghe) witch or old woman

masanéta (plural masanéte) female crab (Carcinus
mediterraneus) (October-November), particularly
sought after when it is carrying eggs

masorìn (plural masorìni) male duck
(October-November), which should not weigh
more than one kilogram

mazzancolla (plural mazzancolle: standard Italian)
shallow-water prawn

moèca (plural moéche) male masanéta (Carcinus
mediterraneus), caught during the moulting period
when the shell is soft and the crab can be eaten whole
(March-April and October-November)

moscardino (plural moscardini: standard Italian)
the Italian for folpéto, or baby octopus

mostarda (standard Italian)
a mixed fruit chutney

mozzarella in carrozza (standard
Italian) a slice of mozzarella
cheese topped with an anchovy,
sandwiched between two slices
of bread, dipped in egg and
then fried

muséto pork sausage similar to Italian cotechino
but made mainly with meat from the muso
(head), steamed or boiled and then served
sliced with potato purée and lentils

muneghéte the Venetian version of pop corn

musso (plural mùssi) donkey

narànza (plural narànza) orange

nervéti veal cartilage boiled and served as cichèti
with onion, parsley, vinegar and oil

nicolòta traditional sweet made from stale bread,
milk, flour, raisins and fennel seeds

novellàme name used for the fry of sea fish only;
the term derives from novèllo, meaning "young"

_87

LATTI DI SEPPIA

GAMBERETTI

CANÒCE

GARÙSOLI

SÉPA ROSTA

GRANSÉOLA

FOLPÉTI

BÌGOLI IN SALSA

POLENTA E BACCALÀ

òcio! look out!

oràda (plural **oràde**) gilthead bream (*Sparus auratus*) (July-September)

oradèlla or **oradìna** (plural **oradèlle, oradìne**) young gilthead bream (*Sparus auratus*)

òstrega (plural **òstreghe**) oyster (*Ostrea edulis*)

ostreghèta! exclamation of surprise

òmbra or **ombréta** (plural **òmbre, ombréte**; literally "shadow") glass of white or red wine drunk standing at the bar, so called because wine was once sold this way at stalls in the shadow of the bell tower of San Marco

osèi scampài (literally, "birds that got away"); skewers of veal, beef or pork with lard, sage and white wine; the name derives from the Venetian habit of serving small birds roasted on a skewer

ossocòlo *coppa* sausage

osteria (plural **osterie**) originally a public house serving wine although most now serve bar food as well; an *osteria con cucina* serves table meals

panàda *venexiana*, or *pan bògio all'ogio;* bread soup flavoured with garlic, oil, bay leaf and parmesan cheese

pancetta (standard Italian) fatty pork belly

panino (plural **panini**: standard Italian) filled roll

panòcia (plural **panòce**) corn cob

pantegàna (plural **pantegàne**) rat

parsèmolo parsley

parsùto ham (standard Italian *prosciutto*)

passarìn (plural **passarìni**) flounder (*Platichtys flesus*) (September-November)

pasticcio (plural **pasticci**: standard Italian) pasta baked in the oven

pastissàda the art of using leftover vegetables, pasta, cold meats and cheese, usually cooked with **polenta**

peòchio (plural **peòci**) mussel (*Mytilus galloprovincialis*) (June-September)

persegàda quince preserve known in Italian as *cotognata*; It is made in the shape of a man on horseback for the feast of St Martin on 11 November

pessenovèllo another name for **novellàme**

peveràda sauce made from stock, breadcrumbs, spices and cheese

pinsa cake made at Epiphany (6 January) from yellow and white flour, fennel seeds, raisins, dried figs and candied peel

SOPPRÈSSA

LUGÀNEGA

88_

PEÒCI GRATINATI

FASIÒI

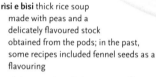

TRIPPE IN UMIDO

piròn (plural **piròni**) fork

polàstro (plural **polàstri**) chicken, also a name for a naive or silly person

polenta (standard Italian) a porridge-like preparation of coarsely ground cornflour served hot, or cooled, sliced and toasted, as an accompaniment for meat or fish

polpetta (plural **polpette**; standard Italian) fried meatball or rissole

pómo (plural **pómi**) apple

porcino (plural **porcini**) the cep or penny bun mushroom (*Boletus edulis*)

pòrtego (plural **pòrteghi**) main upper-floor salon of a house

primo (plural **primi**: standard Italian) a **primo piatto** or "first course" of pasta, rice or soup

prosecco a light, dry or off-dry white wine, sometimes semi-sparkling, made in the province of Treviso

puìna ricotta cheese

putèo (plural **putèi**) male child **putèa** (plural **putèe**) female child

radicchio trevigiano or **radicchio di Treviso** (standard Italian) red-leaf chicory, a specialty of Treviso

ramo minor street leading off a *calle*

rio canal

rio terà (plural **rii terà**) infilled canal

rìsi e bìsi thick rice soup made with peas and a delicately flavoured stock obtained from the pods; in the past, some recipes included fennel seeds as a flavouring

rosàda custard made from eggs, milk and sugar

rumegàl calf's gullet

_89

rùstego (plural **rùsteghi**) or "rustic" is what Venetians call someone who is a little grumpy and apparently unsociable but plain speaking

salizada (standard Italian *selciato*) paved street

sanguèto black pudding made from pig's blood cooked with onion and other flavourings until thick enough to be sliced

saltimbocca (standard Italian) sautéed scallop of veal or chicken

saór marinade made from sliced and fried onions, vinegar, pine nuts and raisins

sardèla (plural **sardèle**) sardine (*Sardina pilchardus*) (June-October); in the well-known Venetian specialty **sardèle in saór**, the sardines are dusted in flour and fried, then marinaded in **saór**

sardòne (plural **sardoni**) anchovies (*Engraulis encrasicholus*) (June-October)

sarèsa (plural **sarèse**) cherry

MUSÉTO

MÈZI VÓVI

BUSSOLÀI
BURANÈI

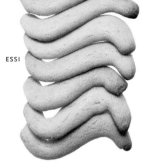

ESSI

BAÌCOLI

schìla (plural **schìe**) small grey shrimp (*Crangon crangon*) common in the lagoon; usually, they are shelled – which takes ages – boiled and dressed, or cooked in a sauce, to be served with **polenta** (October-December)

s'ciopà used to indicate an alternatively coiffeured radical type who smokes suspicious-looking handmade cigarettes and might well ask you for a euro, unless he or she comes from a wealthy family

90_

s'ciòso (plural **s'ciòsi**) snail

scugèr (plural **scugèri**) spoon

sècoe the small pieces of flesh that remain attached to the spine of a butchered steer or calf; used mainly for risottos; once, **sècoe** were the food of the poor but they can now be found in the best restaurants

secondo (plural **secondi**: standard Italian) a **secondo piatto** or "second course"

sègola (plural **sègole**) onion

semifreddo (standard Italian) a type of sweet made by chilling or partially freezing – the name means "half cold" – a custard-like mousse

sépa (plural **sèpe**) cuttlefish (*Sepia officinalis*), traditionally cooked in their ink, are served with **polenta** or as a sauce for risottos or pasta (July-August)

sestière (plural **sestièri**) one of Venice's six administrative districts

sfògio (plural **sfògi**) sole (*Solea vulgaris*) (August-October)

sgropìn sorbet of lemon, vodka and **prosecco**, served at the end of a fish meal

sguassétto alla bechéra rich meat stew (literally, "butcher's stew")

soàso (plural **soàsi**) brill (*Scophthalmus rhombus*) (October)

sòpa coàda soup made of bread and pigeon cooked in the oven

soprèssa (standard Italian *soppressa*) large fresh country salami, sometimes flavoured with garlic

sotopòrtego (plural **sotopòrteghi**) covered passage adjoining a house

spàreso (plural **sparèsi**) asparagus

spiénsa spleen

spritz the Venetian aperitif of white wine with bitter campari, select or aperol and soda

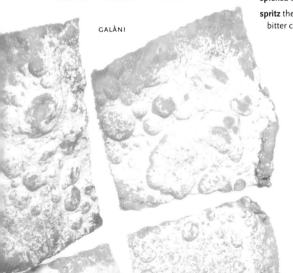

GALÀNI

FRÌTOLE

TIRAMISÙ

spumìlia (plural **spumìlie**) meringues

squèro (plural **squèri**) boatyard where gondolas are made

stracaganàse dried chestnuts (the name means "jaw-strainers")

stròpolo (plural **stròpoli**) bottle top or cork

sùca pumpkin

sùgoli sweet made with American grapes and flour

sùpa soup

tabàro (plural **tabàri**) cloak

tècia low-sided pan or frying pan

tegolìne French beans

testìna calf's head

tetìna cow's udder

tirimesù (or **tiramisù** – the name means "pick-me-up") sweet made with layers of coffee-soaked biscuits, mascarpone cream cheese and eggs, then sprinkled with cocoa powder; the coffee and calories are guaranteed to give anyone a lift

tòcio sauce for dunking; *tociàr* means to dip bread in the sauce

tòco piece

tòla table

torbolìn very young, off-dry wine that is still cloudy; *torbido* is the Italian for "cloudy" (October-November)

tramezzino (plural **tramezzini**: standard Italian)

vàlle (plural **vàlli**) part of the lagoon marked, fenced off or bounded by an embankment, and used for fish farming

vedèlo (plural **vedèli**) calf

viéro (plural **viéri**) floating, usually circular, container used to conserve fish or shellfish temporarily, especially when selecting *moèche*, *spiàntani* and *masanéte*; it is also used for collecting *schìe*

vòvo (plural **vòvi**) egg; half a boiled egg, a *mèso vòvo*, is a popular bar snack

zabaiòn a custard of egg yolk, sugar, cinnamon and sweet fortified wine, known in Italian as *zabaione* or *zabaglione*

zalèto (plural **zalèti**) typical yellow biscuits made with cornflour, sugar, eggs and raisins

zòtolo (plural **zòtoli**) small cuttlefish (*Sepia officinalis*)

ZALÉTI

_91

PINZA

CARAMÈI

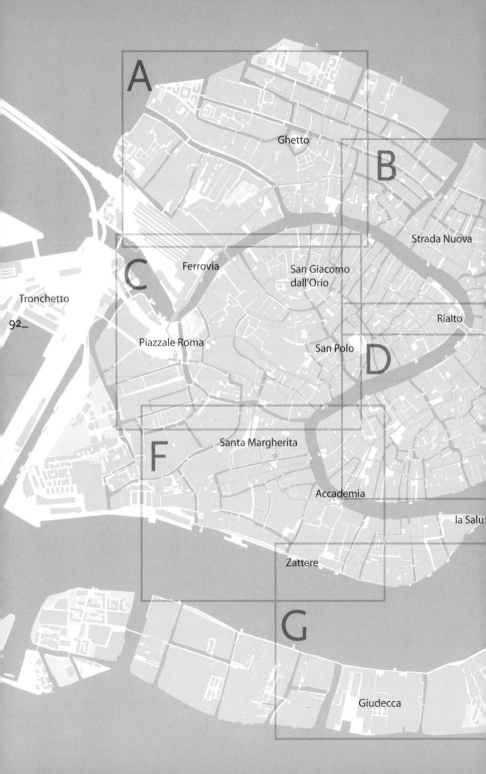

A

Ghetto

B

Strada Nuova

C

Ferrovia

San Giacomo
dall'Orio

Rialto

Tronchetto

92_

Piazzale Roma

San Polo

D

F

Santa Margherita

Accademia

la Salu

Zattere

G

Giudecca

map

Fondamente Nuove

Santi Giovanni e Paolo

E

Santa Maria Formosa

an Marco

Arsenale

Via Garibaldi

H

Giardini della Biennale

San Giorgio

Sant'Elena

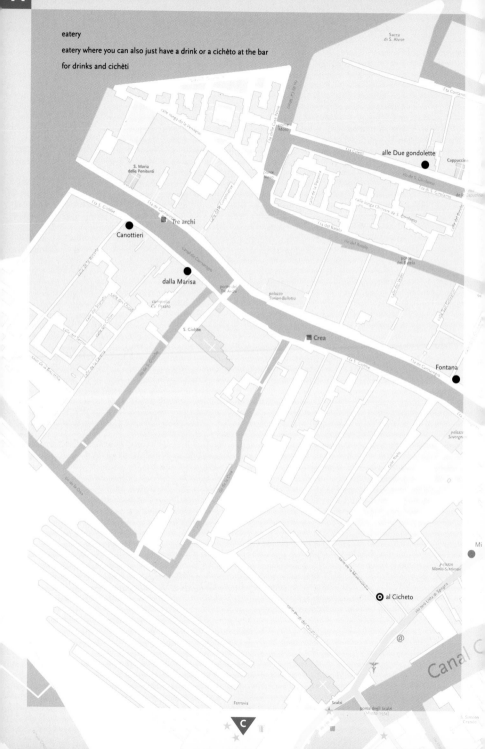

A

eatery

eatery where you can also just have a drink or a cichèto at the bar

for drinks and cichèti

Sacca
di S. Alvise

alle Due gondolette

Cappuccine

S. Maria
delle Penitenti

Tre archi

Canottieri

dalla Marisa

S. Giobbe

Crea

Fontana

palazzo
Savorgna

Mi

al Cicheto

@

Canal C

Ferrovia

Scalzi

ponte degli Scalzi

C

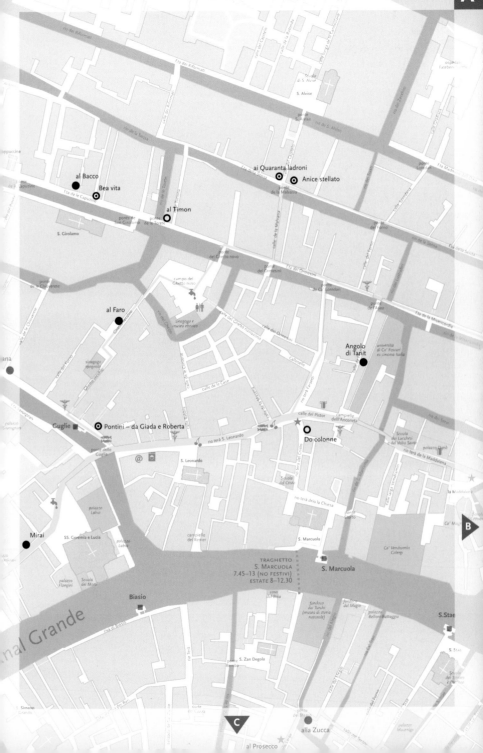

B

Angolo di Tanit

Rioba

Sahara

il Santo bevitore

A

Vini da Gigio

al Fontego dei pescaori

S.Stae

la Cantina

ai Osti

Canal Grande

Ca' d'Oro

Ca' d'Oro

Vecio bragozzo

TRAGHETTO
S. SOFIA
7.30–20.30
FESTIVO 8–19

Antico giardinetto

al Vecio fritoin

al Nono risorto

Muro

da Pinto

Do mori

al Garanghelo (1)

Do spade

Marcà

ai Storti

alla Ciurma

al Bancogiro

C

all'Arco

Naranzaria

da Fiore

Antiche carampane

al Diavolo e
l'acqua santa

Ruga Rialto

alla Madonna

Birraria

D

Rialto

B

Fondamente Nuove

palazzo Donà ● Algiubagiò

● da Alvise

● alla Frasca

coop

● da Bepi – già '54

● Cea

● Boccadoro

⊙ un Mondo divino

⊙ da Alberto

● Tre spiedi – da Bes

⊙ al Ponte

● Fiaschetteria toscana

● Santa Marina

⊙ al Portego

○ aï Rusteghi

⊙ alla Botte

⊙ alla Mascareta

● al Mascaron

⊙ Gislon

E

D

C

A

Canal

Ferrovia

Scalzi

ponte degli Scalzi
(Miozzi 1934)

S. Simeon
Piccolo

Ferrovia

Canal Grande

coop

P. Roma

Scuola
dei Trevisani
del punto di lana

garage Comunale

ponte Santa Lucia
(Calatrava 2007)

ponte
dei Monastero

Rivetta

ponte
de la Croce

Deposito bagagli
aperto tutti i giorni (7-21)

giardin Papadopoli

calle de Ca' Amai

pont
de la Pescheria

Iuav

ponte
del Prefetto

ponte
dei Tolentini

Tolentini

da Lele

Wine bar

piazzale Roma

ponte
de S. Andrea

Tre ponti

ponte
del Magazen

ponte
de Gaffaro

Scuola
dei Lanai

ponte de
la strada S. Pantalon

ponte de
Cal Marcello

ae Cravate

ria de le Burchiele

ria tera S. Boldo

ponte
de la Cereria

corte de
Ca' Storlan

pont
de la Sblaca

calle Nova

S. Maria Maggiore

ponte
de Rioba

calle del Forno

Ca' Foscolo-Con

F

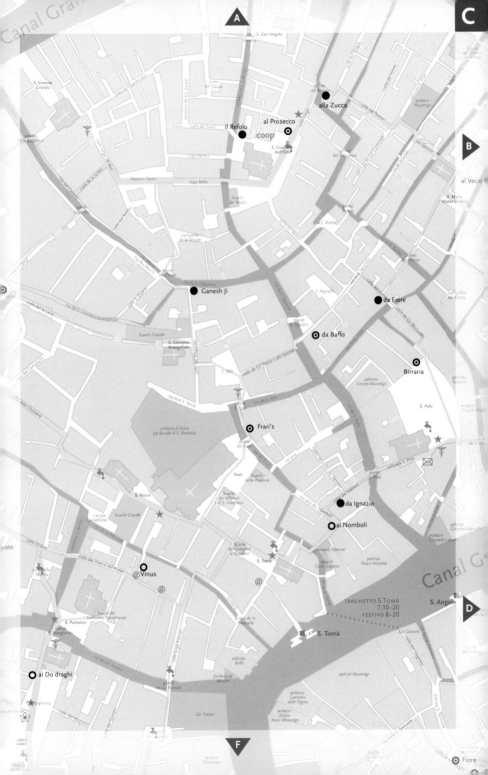

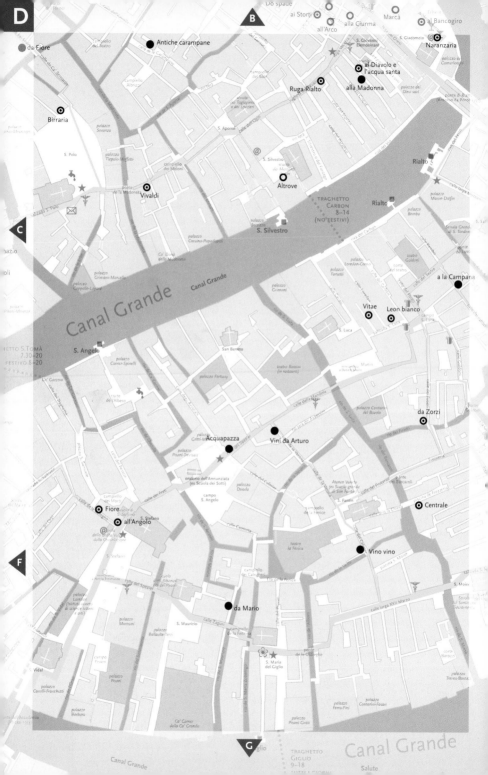

Celestia

Scuola di
S. Pasquale Baylon

campo de ti Celestia

sede università

archivio storico
delle Celestia

calle del Forno

campo
de le Pegola

pointe
del Cavallino

campo
S. Ternita

rio de la Celestia

calle Drio

calle del Cimitero

calle de le Celatele

darsena vecchia

rio de le Gorne

Arsenale

campo
De i Pozzi

darsena nuova

calle de le Gorne

campo
de le Gorne

rio de la Tana

pointe
de la Chiesa

pointe
S. Martin

S. Martin

t.ta de fazza de l'Arsenal

campo
de l'Arsenal

Corte sconta

Scuola di
S. Marina

calle de la Nave

salizada del Pignater

campo
del Paradiso

Fubera

t.ta de l'Arsenal

Ca' di Dio

rio de l'Arsenal

campo de la Tana

calle de la Tana

t.ta de la Tana

pointe
de la Ca' di Dio

Museo storico
navale

calle Cabotto

S. Francesco
di Paola

Arsenale

pointe
de l'Arsenal

S. Biagio

rio S. Biagio

Angiò

via Garibaldi

al Garanghélo (2)

calle Cabotto

pointe
de la Veneta Marina

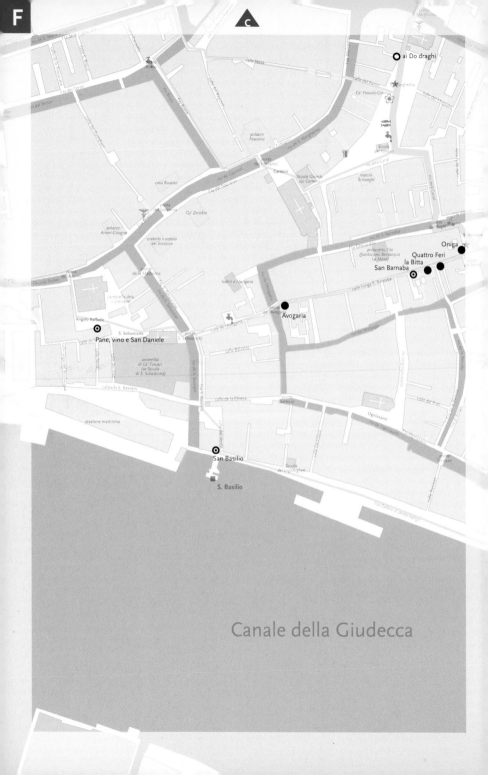

F

ai Do draghi

Oniga

Quattro Feri

la Bitta

San Barnaba

Avogaria

Pane, vino e San Daniele

San Basilio

S. Basilio

Canale della Giudecca

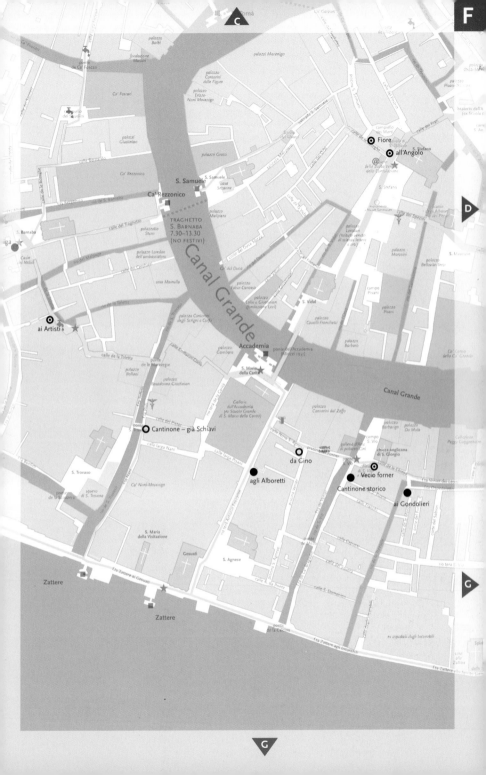

F

C

Tomà

palazzo
Balbi

fondamenta
Minich

pont
de Cà Foscari

palazzo
de Cà Foscari

Ca' Foscari

palazzi
Giustinian

Ca' Rezzonico

palazzetto
Stern

palazzo Loredan
dell'ambasciatore

palazzi Consorzi
delle Figure

palazzo
Erizzo
Nani Mocenigo

palazzo Grassi

S. Samuele

S. Samuele

Ca' Rezzonico

casa
Serpana

palazzo
Malipiero

**TRAGHETTO
S. BARNABA
7.30–13.30
(NO FESTIVI)**

calle del Traghetto

calle del Teatro

palazzetto
Stern

palazzo Loredan
dell'ambasciatore

casa Mamuli

palazzo Loredan
(museo vendita
di scienza lettere
e arti)

Canal Grande

campiello
dei Morti

Scuola a
S. Stefano

S. Stefano

@ all'Angolo

◎ Fiore

Scuola Vera
della Carità
delle Contarini

S. Stefano

campo
S. Maurizio

S. Maurizio

palazzo
Bellavitis Terzi

S. Barnaba

iga

Casin
del Nobil

calle de la Toletta

S. Maria
della Carità

palazzo Cavalli-Franchetti

campo
Pisani

palazzo
Pisani

ponte de la Toletta

palazzetto
Giustinian-Recanati

palazzo Barbaro

Ca' Corner
della Ca' Granda

⊙★ ai Artisti

palazzo
Contarini
agli Scrigni e Corfù

Accademia

ponte de l'Accademia
(Miozzi 1933)

Cà del Duca

palazzo
Falier-Canossa

palazzo
Colin e Giustinian
(pondazione e Levi)

S. Vidal

palazzo
Cavalli-Franchetti

Canal Grande

palazzo Barbarigo

palazzo
Da Mula

palazzo
Barbaro

ponte
de la Maravegie

calle de la Toletta

palazzo
Bollani

palazzo
Brandolin-Giustinian

Galleria
dell'Accademia
(ex Scuola Grande
di S. Maria della Carità)

palazzo
Contarini dal Zaffo

collezione
Peggy Guggenheim

○ Cantinone – già Schiavi

calle Nova S. Agnese

calle d'Ar
di palazzo Cini

chiesa anglicana
di S. Giorgio

○ da Gino

piscina forner

campo
S. Vio

S. Vio

Rio Venier dei Leoni

calle larga Nani

calle larga Pisani

Ca' Nani-Mocenigo

● agli Alboretti

S. Trovaso

squero
di S. Trovaso

ponte
de S. Trovaso

S. Maria
della Visitazione

Gesuati

S. Agnese

● Vecio forner

● ★
Cantinone storico

● ai Gondolieri

ramo
Calcina

calle Cipriani

rio tera Antonio Foscarini

Zattere

Fta Zattere ai Gesuati

Zattere

ponte
de la Calcina

calle E. Danieli

ponte
S. Domenico

calle S. Domenico

calle e S. Vio

calle e da Ponte

★

G

ex ospedale degli Incurabili

Fta Zattere agli Incurabili

Fta Zattere allo Spirito

vaco
alla
Zattera

G

G

F

F
Zattere

S. Maria
della Visitazione

Gesuati

S. Agnese

S. Zattere ai Gesuati

ai Gondolieri

calle Capuzzi

calle del Pistor

no tera S. Vio

ponte
de Mezo

calle A. da Ponte

Pozzo di Ferro

calle S. Domenico

er ospedale degli Incurabili

Spirito Santo

casa allo Zottiere

Scuola dello Spirito Santo

Zattere

ponte
de la Calcina

S.ta Zattere agli Incurabili

S.ta Zattere allo Spirito Santo

Canale della Giudecca

Giudecca

alla Palanca

coop

S.ta del Ponte Piccolo

Ponte Longo

Altanella

Casino Biffo

Redentore

S. Biondetto

campo
S. Giacomo

S.ta S. Giacomo

Campiello Ferranda

S.ta de la Palada

S.ta del Ponte Longo

calle de Frene

Corte canonica minore

calle de la Mare

Calle del Prvae

calle de l'Albero

calle dei Orti

Mistrà

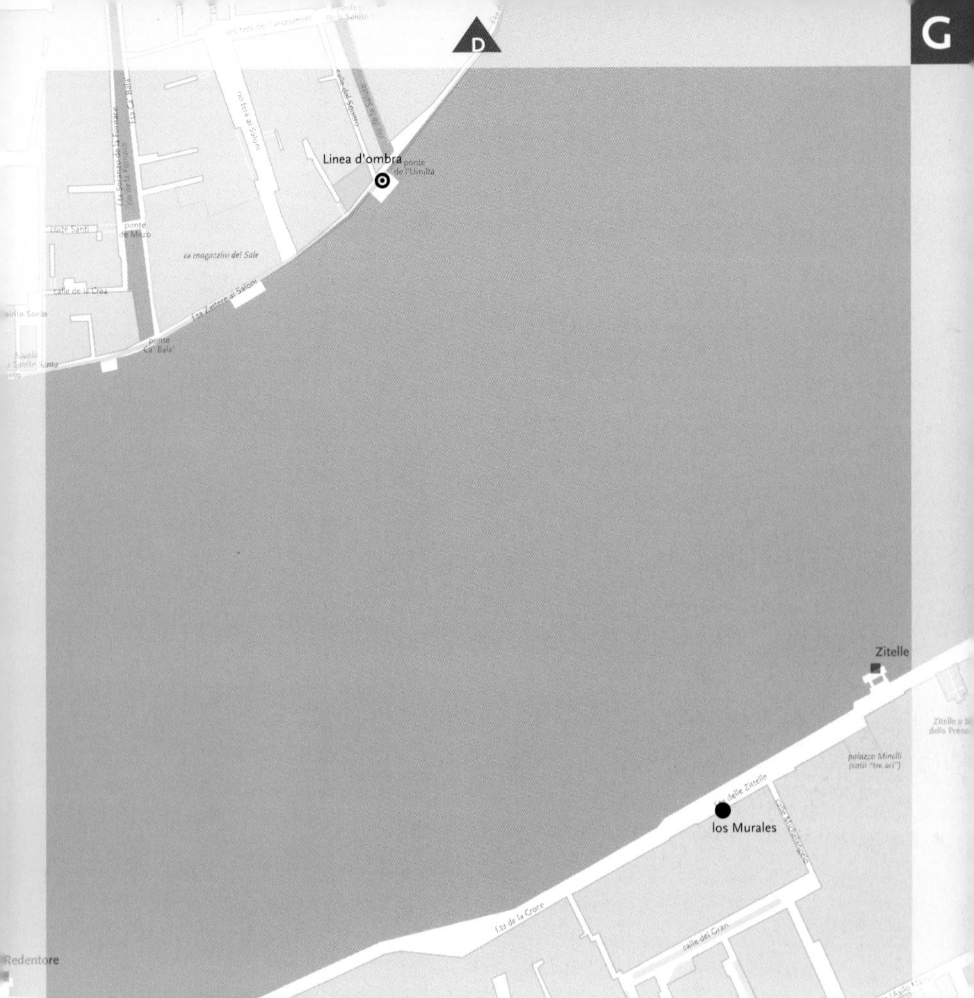

Linea d'ombra *ponte de l'Umiltà*

ex magazzino del Sale

Zitelle

Zitelle o Si... della Prese...

palazzo Minelli (casa "tre ari")

calle Zitelle

los Murales

F.ta de la Croce

Redentore

S. Redentore *ponte de la Croce*

Santa Croce

Tre scaini

lo (2)

ai Tosi piccoli

Giardini

gondola-ferry stop
The Grand Canal can be crossed at seven points in
gondola-ferries for 40 cents. The service is still much
patronised by Venetians

chemist's (9 am–12.30 pm and 3.45 pm–7.30 pm)
open during week and Saturday afternoon and Sunday
on a rota system

fountain with drinking water

newsstand (7 am–6 pm)
open Monday to Saturday and Sunday on a rota system

fish stall
open Tuesday to Saturday, mornings only

fruit and vegetable stall
open Tuesday to Saturday, mornings only

flower stall
open Tuesday and Saturday, mornings only

post office

token-operated laundry

ATM

cooperativa trasbagagli Piazzale Roma
041 5223590

left luggage
041 5231107, open every day (6 am–9 pm)

coop   coop supermarket

@   internet point

Sant'Elena

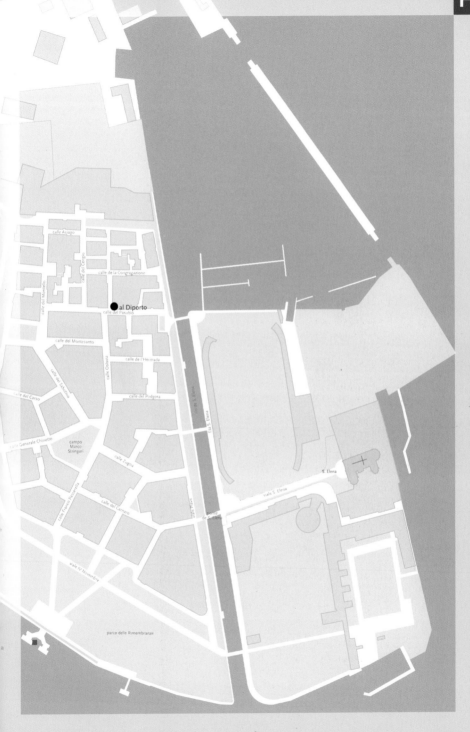

calle Avuago
calle del Cengio
calle de la Congregazione
calle del Montello
● al Diporto
calle del Pasubio
calle del Montesanto
calle de l'Hermada
calle Oslavia
calle del Cadore
Calle del Carso
calle del Podgora
calle Generale Chinotto
campo Marco Stringari
calle Zsigna
calle Franco Pasarela
Calle del Carnaro
viale IV Novembre
isola S. Elena
calle de S. Elena
viale S. Elena
S. Elena
ponte de S. Elena
parco delle Rimembranze

Printed in February 2006, at Grafiche Vianello, Ponzano/Treviso.